The origins of the cat family can be traced back more th[an]
years ago. Ancient ancestors evolved (developed) into ei[ther]
or generations, of cats, with all of them shown here.

Leopard cat

The Leopard cat lineage split off 6.2 MYA with a group including the fishing cat, rusty-spotted cat, and Pallas's cat.

Fishing cat

Pallas's cat

Puma

The puma, jaguarundi, and cheetah are among the members of the Puma lineage from 6.7 MYA.

Puma

Cheetah

Felis

The most recent lineage evolved 3.4 MYA to categorise lighter cats weighing less than 10 kg (22 lb).

Wild

Smaller wild cats, including the black-footed cat, sand cat, and jungle cat, all belong to the Felis lineage.

Black-footed cat

Domestic

The Felis lineage also includes the many different breeds of domestic cat found around the world.

Maine Coon cat

Things to find out:

Contents

Introduction

I've been fond of food from an early age, but mostly Indian food, and I've always loved cooking. My earliest memory of being in the kitchen was when my grandmother bought me a small rolling pin and board to help her make the rotis for the family dinner. She pronounced, 'If you can make them round, you will find a good husband', and as a little girl I thought this was rather strange. But day after day I would sit with my board and pin, concentrating on trying to get my rotis perfectly round. This was our time together, and I'll never forget how much care she took in helping me find my love of cooking.

My parents were busy growing our family food business into the global household brand they always hoped for, and I spent every holiday at the office learning the tricks of the trade. My mum would bring home recipes she had been experimenting with and test them out on my brothers and me. If we liked them, they would find their way into a jar and on to the supermarket shelf. My parents made sure we were exposed to a wide variety of flavours from all corners of the world, and little did I know that I was training my taste buds for a life in food.

'I grew up in a spice-loving family where spice not only dominated our dishes but was usually the topic of conversation around the table.'

Spices are magical ingredients that have the ability to transform a dish from ordinary into extraordinary. Spices are big, bold and vibrant, exploding in your mouth and making you feel alive. Although this experience isn't for everyone, when I first tasted Indian food I was hooked and instantly understood that adding a few spices to some simple ingredients can create delicious results. I was lucky enough to eat incredible food at home. Coming from a whole generation of accomplished cooks, we loved to stay in, cook and then eat as a family rather than going out. Traditional Indian food made by my grandmother or experimental Asian cooking by my mum was what I regarded as the norm. When I left home to study at uni, I realized it was rare to have grown up cooking at home to that creative level. Those early cooking lessons are ones I will cherish forever.

In putting this book together, I wanted to draw on the food I love and have loved growing up. The dishes I've included are all inspired by the special food encounters I've experienced and the wonderful flavours and ingredients I've discovered along the way. From our Sunday roast family favourite Slow-roast Spiced Lamb (*see* page 44) to my dad's Smokin' Ribs (*see* page 132), which we have only once a year, all my recipes hold a special place in my heart.

Throughout my life, and as a result of my travels and my experiences, my confidence in using spices has grown. My professional culinary training at Leiths School of Food and Wine in London taught me techniques I'd never used before, and I've embraced many new ingredients, flavours and ideas from around the world to help bring out the enchanting qualities of spices. I wanted to offer a good balance of recipes between light, uplifting dishes that you can ease into your busy life, and a few long, slow-cooked ones designed to intensify those luscious Indian flavours; recipes for those rushed days when cooking needs to be especially quick, along with some for sun-filled barbecue get-togethers, showstopper dinner party mains and the health-conscious in need of nutritious, feel-good dishes. The Sugar & Spice section has the most recipes, as I have a sweet tooth just like my father and go crazy for desserts.

Scattered throughout the recipes are My Secret stamps giving you tips on how to make the most of your ingredients, ways to tweak the recipes for slightly different yet still scrumptious results, and some of my favourite serving suggestions. I also simply had to share some of my secret kitchen essentials with you, including a peek into my Everyday Spice Box (*see* pages 36–41) and Storecupboard Must-haves (*see* pages 68–9),

'The best recipes only taste the best because they are filled with emotion, filled with love. They come from precious memories, and all have a story to tell.'

'This book isn't for those wanting to learn traditional Indian cooking, but for those who love the spice flavours characteristic of Indian food and want to be shown how to use them in exciting and unexpected ways.'

which Kitchen Gadgets I rely on (*see* pages 110–11), how to make the most of Magical Chillies (*see* pages 88–9) and my Wine & Spice guide (*see* pages 214–5).

Indian food is usually seen as complicated with seemingly endless ingredient lists, but I wanted to share recipes with you that won't take forever and don't need a truckload of ingredients. A well-stocked storecupboard is all you need, and if you don't have one of the items listed, don't worry about it – simply leave it out, use your intuition and the end result will taste great.

I'm particularly passionate about bringing out the cook and food lover within each and every one of us, and I have sought to feature recipes that will both inspire those who love to cook as well as entice and satisfy those who love to eat. I want my recipes to be used as a canvas for experimenting with flavours. That's the way I love to cook, with my pantry wide open so that I can see what I have to play with. But my desire to eat well will always lead my taste buds back to the spice flavours of home, and my family who helped me discover my great love of food.

'I believe that cooking should be a pleasurable experience and approached with an adventurous mind.'

I have always believed that good cookbooks should be covered in splashes from the preparation of meals gone by, and full of the cook's own scribbled substitutions and suggestions. They should look dog-eared and crinkled from being well read and frequently cooked from. That's what I hope for my cookbook… a book that is loved and used for many years to come.

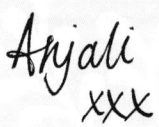

CHAPTER

1

LIGHT
BITES

SERVES 4
(MAKES ABOUT 12)
Prep time 10 minutes
Cook time 5 minutes if
cooking in a single batch

vegetable oil, for frying – you won't
need more than 1 litre (1³/4 pints)
2 carrots
1 large red onion
3cm (1¹/4in) piece fresh root
ginger, peeled
good handful of spinach leaves,
roughly chopped
1 red chilli, finely chopped
2 tbsp roughly chopped
fresh coriander

1 tsp cumin seeds
1 tsp ground turmeric
1 tsp garam masala
¹/2 tsp ground asafoetida/hing
(optional)
juice of 1 lemon
good pinch of salt
100g (3¹/2oz) gram (chickpea)
flour (see My Secret, below)

Carrot, onion & spinach bhajias

Bhajias will always hold a special place in my heart. When my grandparents moved to the UK in the 1950s they were incredibly poor, so they had to do whatever they could to keep themselves afloat and provide for my dad and his siblings. My grandmother did what she loved, which was cooking. Her Indian samosas, bhajias and traditional desserts gained national fame, and from these humble beginnings the Patak's brand was born. My granny loved being in the kitchen and she taught me more about Gujarati cooking than I could ever thank her for. This is actually not one of her recipes but more of a modern spin on an old classic.

Pour vegetable oil into a large, deep-lipped frying pan so that it comes 5cm (2in) up the sides. Gently heat it while you prepare the bhajia mixture. Alternatively, heat a deep-fat fryer to 180°C/350°F.

Grate the carrots, onion and ginger using a cheese grater. Transfer them to a large bowl and add the rest of the ingredients. Scrunch all of the mixture together with your hands to release the moisture from the veggies and help it bind together. If you need to, add a few tablespoons of water – you want it to be a dropping consistency. Shape the mixture into balls of around a tablespoonful each before flattening them a little, which allows them to cook all the way through so that they don't end up with a doughy centre.

Add a little of the mixture to the oil to test if it's hot enough: it should sink and then swim. Deep-fry the bhajias, in batches if you need to, for about 5 minutes until they are golden brown. You will need to flip them a few times to get an even colour. Drain on kitchen paper.

Serve hot with Mango Chutney (see page 167) or your favourite dip.

· MY SECRET ·
Gram flour, made from ground
chickpeas, is used widely in Indian
cooking and is gluten free. It can
be found in most supermarkets.
If you don't have any to hand,
use plain flour instead and add
a little more turmeric to give
the bhajias a good colour.

SERVES 4
Prep time 20 minutes
Cook time 5 minutes

8 courgette flowers with baby
    courgettes attached (preferably),
    flower stamens removed
2 tbsp vegetable oil
good drizzle of clear honey
1 red chilli, deseeded and
    finely chopped

Stuffing
3 tbsp ricotta cheese
1 garlic clove, finely chopped
$^1/_2$ tbsp finely chopped chives
$^1/_2$ tbsp pine nuts, toasted and finely
    chopped, plus extra to garnish
pinch of ground green
    cardamom (optional)

Stuffed courgette flowers with ricotta & honey

Courgette flowers are seen as exotic and are only available when courgettes come into season. They have a light, subtle flavour and so I'm adding sweet spices to my ricotta with just a little chilli heat to help the honey taste even sweeter. This is a great starter to any meal.

Mix all the stuffing ingredients together in a bowl.

Slit the courgettes through the middle lengthways but not all the way to the top so that the heat from the pan can cook them all the way through. Carefully stuff the flowers with the ricotta stuffing, trying not to overfill them. Twist the top to seal.

Gently heat the oil in a large frying pan and pan-fry the flowers for a few minutes until they are light golden brown on all sides. Transfer the flowers to a plate, draining on kitchen paper if you need to, and drizzle with honey. Sprinkle over the chilli and a few extra toasted pine nuts to garnish.

· MY SECRET ·
Courgette flowers are delicate.
Be careful when stuffing them to
avoid damaging the petals. If you
can get hold of baby courgettes
with the flowers still attached,
then great, otherwise the
flowers alone will do.

SERVES 4 AS A SNACK
Prep time 5 minutes
Cook time 3 minutes if
cooking in a single batch

3 tbsp vegetable oil or light olive
   oil, plus extra if needed
200g (7oz) okra, thinly sliced
2 tbsp gram (chickpea) flour
   or plain flour
1 tsp ground turmeric
1/2 tsp chilli powder
1 tbsp ground sumac
pinch of sea salt, or to taste

Crispy sumac okra

Frying okra makes this otherwise slimy vegetable taste absolutely wonderful. The sticky texture disappears and it becomes one of the best snacks you'll ever try. In India they would make a spice mix to dust on the okra before frying, but instead of following tradition I have opted for sumac as my flavouring of choice. It's a Middle Eastern spice made from beautiful dried crimson berries that have a sweet, sour and almost lemony flavour. Sumac is now widely available, but you can always substitute your favourite garam masala if you can't find it, although it doesn't have the same flavour. Try and cut the okra all the same size to ensure that they crisp up together without some of them burning.

Heat the oil in a large, shallow frying pan. Sprinkle the okra with the flour, turmeric and chilli powder, and toss together well so that they are all evenly coated.

Test the temperature of the oil by dropping in a little pinch of flour – it should sizzle. Add the okra to the pan and fry for a few minutes, moving them around frequently, until they are light golden brown and crispy. Be careful, as they burn easily, so turn down the heat if you need to. Depending on the size of your pan, you may need to do this in batches, so add a little more oil when frying each batch.

Drain on kitchen paper and sprinkle over the sumac with a good pinch of sea salt. Taste and adjust the flavourings if you need to. Serve hot with a chilled drink for a wonderful party snack.

· MY SECRET ·
I was always taught
never to wash okra,
as they absorb water,
so instead I wipe them
with a damp cloth
to clean them.

SERVES 4
Prep time 5 minutes
Cook time 15 minutes

10 baby aubergines, cut in half
and flesh scored with a cross
2 tbsp vegetable oil

Stuffing
2 tsp black mustard seeds
2 tsp peeled and finely chopped
fresh root ginger
1–2 red chillies, finely chopped

15 fresh curry leaves
4 heaped tbsp desiccated
coconut
3 tbsp chopped chives
pinch of salt, or to taste

To finish
2 tbsp natural yogurt
clear honey, for drizzling

Charred baby aubergines

*My grandmother used to
make a dish just like this when
I was young. She used large
aubergines but I prefer baby
ones as they are just the right
size for snacking when they are
halved lengthways. If you do
use large ones, make sure you
roast them for longer.*

Preheat your grill to medium, preferably an oven grill if you have
one, or the oven to 220°C/425°F/Gas Mark 7. Rub the aubergines
with half the oil and grill or roast, cut-side down. The skin should
start to change colour and turn crispy after 10–15 minutes.

In the meantime, make the stuffing. Gently heat the remaining
oil in a small frying pan and add the mustard seeds. When the
seeds start to jump out of the pan, add the ginger, chillies and curry
leaves and allow to cook for 1 minute before stirring in the coconut.
This should start to toast and turn golden brown after around
30 seconds. Turn off the heat and add half the chives and a pinch
of salt. Stir well and taste and adjust the seasoning if you need to.

Remove the aubergines from the grill or oven and flip them over so
that you can see the flesh side. Fill the aubergines with the stuffing.
Drizzle with the yogurt and some honey, and sprinkle over the
remaining chives before serving.

· MY SECRET ·
Fresh curry leaves must
be thoroughly rinsed under
cold running water before use.
Available at Asian stores and
large supermarkets, curry
leaves freeze well. Buy a large
bag and use from frozen
whenever a recipe
calls for them.

SERVES 4 AS A SNACK
Prep time 10 minutes
Cook time 5 minutes

400g (14oz) cleaned squid,
  cut into small bite-sized pieces
milk, for soaking
vegetable oil, for frying
5 tbsp plain flour
1 tsp ajwain seeds (optional)
1/2 tsp ground turmeric
1/4 tsp ground asafoetida/hing
  (optional)

2 spring onions, finely chopped
2 garlic cloves, finely chopped
1 red chilli, deseeded if you
  wish, finely chopped
20 fresh curry leaves
  (see My Secret, page 20)
juice of 1 lime
salt and pepper

Flash-fried calamari

Fried squid wins the hearts of most people and I'm one of them. As much as I like the usual sprinkling of salt and citrus, I'm going for something different here. I've fried up some spring onions, garlic, chilli and curry leaves to toss through, and it tastes awesome!

I'm using the tried-and-trusted tenderizing technique of soaking the squid in milk. It tastes best if you can leave it for a few hours, but in this recipe I only do it for 5 minutes while I get on with the chopping. Something is better than nothing.

Soak the squid in milk, making sure it is completely covered, while you prepare the other ingredients.

Pour vegetable oil into a large, deep-lipped frying pan so that it comes 2cm (3/4 in) up the sides and put on to heat. Alternatively, heat a deep-fat fryer to 200°C/400°F.

Put the flour in a large bowl and stir in the ajwain seeds (if using), turmeric, asafoetida/hing (if using) and a really good pinch of salt and pepper. Drain the squid and toss in the flour mixture.

Test the temperature of the oil by dropping in a little pinch of flour – it should sizzle. Once the oil is hot enough, dust off any excess flour and carefully deep-fry the squid, in batches, for 1 minute – any longer and it will be rubbery. Drain on kitchen paper.

In the meantime, prepare the flavourings to sprinkle over the calamari. Gently heat 1 tablespoon vegetable oil in a small frying pan, stir in the spring onions, garlic, chilli and curry leaves and fry for 1 minute.

Spoon the fried mixture all over the hot calamari, squeeze over the lime juice and sprinkle with a little more salt before serving.

8 mini or 4 large soft, flour tortilla wraps

Mini tortillas

Now I know this is a Mexican classic, but who doesn't love tortillas? And I couldn't write a cookbook without including some of my favourite recipes. I've used shop-bought tortilla wraps here, but you can make your own if you like, and they aren't that difficult to do. I actually prefer the ready-made ones.

These are some of my favourite tortilla fillings. Make just one or cook them all up, pile separate bowls in the middle of the table and top your tortillas with whatever you like. Sprinkle with finely sliced red onions, jalapeños and some soured cream or yogurt for a true feast. Roll up and devour: no cutlery allowed!

Prep time 10 minutes
Cook time 1¹/₂ hours for chicken, or up to 3 hours for pork

1 onion, sliced
2 bay leaves
6 bone-in chicken thighs, skin removed, or 500g (1lb 2oz) boneless pork shoulder, skin and all the fat removed
2 tbsp tomato purée
1 tbsp tomato ketchup or barbecue sauce
1 tbsp chipotle chilli paste
2 garlic cloves, finely chopped
1 tbsp light brown sugar
2 tsp smoked paprika
juice of 1 orange
200ml (7fl oz) chicken or vegetable stock

Pulled chicken or pork

Preheat the oven to 150°C/300°F/Gas Mark 2.

Lay the onion and bay leaves in the base of a small roasting tray, one that will fit the chicken or pork snugly. Place the meat on top.

Make the marinade by mixing together all the remaining ingredients. Pour over the meat, cover tightly with foil and slow cook in the oven for about 90 minutes for chicken, or up to 3 hours for pork, basting the meat every now and again, until cooked through and falling off the bone.

Shred the meat and mix into the sauce. If the sauce isn't thick enough, you can put the meat aside to keep warm while you reduce it in a saucepan on the hob.

Roast corn salsa

Prep time 10 minutes
Cook time 10 minutes

1 tbsp vegetable oil
200g (7oz) sweetcorn, drained if
    canned or defrosted if frozen
1 tsp cumin seeds
2 garlic cloves, finely chopped
1 red chilli, deseeded if you
    wish, sliced
1 spring onion, finely sliced
good pinch of sea salt, or to taste
grated rind and juice of 1 lime
3 cherry tomatoes, cut into
    quarters (optional)
freshly chopped mint, to garnish

Gently heat a large frying pan, add the oil and sweetcorn and give it a good stir. Turn up the heat and allow the corn to cook until golden brown. Be careful, as the kernels will start to jump out of the pan.

Stir in the cumin seeds, garlic, chilli, spring onion, salt and the lime juice. Allow to cook for a few minutes before stirring in the tomatoes (if using).

Taste and adjust the seasoning if you need to, then garnish with the lime rind and mint.

Avocado & coriander salsa

Prep time 5 minutes

2 ripe avocados, mashed
    lightly with a fork
juice of $1/2$ lime
1 spring onion, roughly chopped
1 red chilli, deseeded and
    finely chopped
1 tbsp roughly chopped
    fresh coriander
good pinch of sea salt
crumbled feta cheese,
    to garnish (optional)

Mix all the ingredients together in a serving bowl and top with a little feta cheese (if using), in which case, remember to go easy on the salt, as the feta will be salty.

Chickpea salsa

Prep time 10 minutes

240g (8 $1/2$oz) can
    chickpeas, drained
2 tbsp light olive oil
1 green chilli, roughly chopped
1 roasted red pepper, deseeded
    and roughly chopped
1 tbsp roughly chopped
    fresh coriander
1 tbsp roughly chopped mint
1 tsp coriander seeds,
    toasted (optional)
$1/2$ red onion, roughly chopped
good pinch of sea salt, or to taste
juice of $1/2$ lime, or to taste

Place all the ingredients in a food processor and pulse a few times until almost smooth – add some water if you need to. Taste and adjust the seasoning.

SERVES 4
Prep time 5 minutes, plus
(preferably) marinating
Cook time 35–40 minutes

12 chicken wings

Hot pepper marinade
2 dried red chillies or a good
    pinch of chilli powder
1 tsp fennel seeds
1 tsp cumin seeds
1 tsp coriander seeds
1 tsp black peppercorns
1 tbsp peeled and roughly
    chopped fresh root ginger
2 garlic cloves, peeled
1 spring onion, roughly chopped
1 tbsp tamarind paste/concentrate

$1/2$ tbsp clear honey
good pinch of ground cinnamon
good pinch of sea salt
1 tbsp vegetable oil

Tandoori marinade
4 tbsp natural yogurt
1 tbsp garlic paste
2 tsp ginger paste
1 tsp ground turmeric
$1/2$–1 tsp chilli powder
2 tsp garam masala
good pinch of sea salt

Spiced chicken wings

My love for wings comes from many school holidays spent in the US visiting family. We would eat them nearly every day – which sounds excessive but we absolutely loved them, and I still do. This isn't a shy dish, so roll up your sleeves and get stuck in. These spiced wings really are finger-licking good. You can tone down the heat or dial it up, depending on what you feel like.

I spent some time learning the regional cuisine in an area of South India called Chettinad. This Hot Pepper Marinade is inspired by my travels, and it's aromatic and punchy with a good hit of spice. I've added in one of my favourite ingredients, tamarind, but you can leave it out if you haven't got any.

Hot pepper wings

Gently heat a heavy-based frying pan and toast the dry spices for a few minutes until fragrant and the seeds are golden brown.

Transfer to a mortar and allow to cool for a few minutes, then roughly grind with a pestle. Add the ginger, garlic and spring onion, and bash together to form a paste. Toss in the rest of the ingredients and taste – the marinade should be slightly sweet, sour and full of flavour.

Rub the marinade over the wings in a dish, cover and leave to marinate in the fridge for a few hours if you can.

Preheat the oven to 200°C/400°F/Gas Mark 6 and heat up a griddle pan, if you have one, over a medium heat. This will get a nice char on the wings before you pop them in the oven to fully cook through.

Chargrill the wings in the griddle pan for a few minutes on each side before transferring to the oven and cooking for a further 30 minutes, or a few minutes longer if not pre-chargrilled. Check they are cooked through before diving in and serving with a relish (*see pages 160–9*).

Tandoori wings

Mix all the ingredients for the marinade together and rub all over the wings in a dish. Marinate, cook and serve as above.

My grandfather (right), Lakshmishankar, fondly known as LG, or Bapuji to me, with Dhiru Mama, Baa's brother (centre) at 134 Drummond Street, London. Indians from all over would travel to the capital to stock up on Bapuji's imported spices, lentils, rices, pulses and homemade Bombay mix. Demand and community spirit was high.

My grandmother (right), Shanta, respectfully known as Baa, cooking up yet another batch of her famous jalebis. Queues for Baa's authentic sweets were long. My Dad and his brothers were soon kept busy delivering parcels all over London (making the most of the free Tube travel for Under 11's).

Baa at Allcroft Road, Kentish Town – this was the first home Baa and Bapuji rented upon arriving in London from Kenya in 1956. Baa would cook up sweets in the tiny kitchen here, sales of which led to the opening of the Drummond Sreet grocery store. Thus, Patak's was born.

Baa (pictured) and Bapuji invest in a van
to keep up with delivery demands following
the opening of the Drummond Street store!

Dad takes a break from making deliveries
to pose with his beloved guitar.

SERVES 4
(MAKES ABOUT 16)
Prep time 10 minutes
Cook time 25 minutes

100g (3½oz) potatoes (any variety), roughly chopped into small pieces
1 tsp ground turmeric
200g (7oz) puff pastry, 5mm (¼in) thick, cut out 16 discs around 5cm (2in) in diameter
1 tbsp vegetable oil
1 tsp black mustard seeds
¼ tsp ground asafoetida/hing (optional)
1 red chilli, deseeded if you wish, finely chopped
1 tsp garam masala

juice of ½ lemon
sea salt

Topping
1 tsp cumin seeds
4 tbsp thick natural yogurt
4 tbsp Sticky Sweet Date Chutney (*see page 168*)
½ small red onion, finely chopped
2 tbsp roughly chopped fresh coriander
seeds of 1 pomegranate (optional)
2 tbsp sev (optional)

Papri chaat

Chaat is the name of a whole host of dishes that are eaten on the streets of India. They are utterly delicious and can vary from one street vendor to the next. This is my recipe for papri chaat, which is traditionally made with potatoes and chickpeas and smothered in yogurt, something sweet and salty (often Sticky Sweet Date Chutney – see page 168) and some crispy gram noodles called sev (as found in Bombay mix). All of this sits on cute little fried pastry discs that can be served warm or cold. To make it authentic is quite tricky, especially if you don't have all the ingredients, so I've made a few short cuts. For instance, life is too short to make your own pastry and so I have used the shop-bought variety, but by all means make your own.

Preheat the oven to 200°C/400°F/Gas Mark 6.

Fill a saucepan with cold water, add the potatoes with half the turmeric and some salt and bring to the boil. Cook until soft (around 10 minutes). Once cooked, drain well.

In the meantime, lay the pastry discs on a baking sheet lined with nonstick baking paper. Place another sheet of baking paper and a baking sheet on top to stop them puffing up. Bake until golden brown on both sides (around 10 minutes). Keep an eye on them, as they colour quickly.

Gently heat a heavy-based frying pan and toast the cumin seeds for a few minutes until golden brown and fragrant. Pour into a mortar, allow to cool for a few minutes, then roughly crush with a pestle.

Heat the oil in a saucepan and add the mustard seeds, asafoetida/hing (if using) and the remaining turmeric. Once sizzling, stir in the chilli, cooked potatoes and garam masala. Using a fork, roughly mash the potatoes into the spices. Squeeze over the lemon juice and season with a pinch of salt. After a few minutes the spices will have cooked through, so give it a taste and adjust the seasoning.

Put the potatoes to one side to cool a little, and also allow the puff pastry discs to cool down before putting it all together.

Start by laying out the puff pastry discs. Top with a heaped teaspoon of the spiced potato and then a good dollop of the yogurt and chutney. Scatter over the onion, coriander, pomegranate and sev (if using), and add a good sprinkling of the toasted cumin.

SERVES 4 AS A SNACK
Prep time 10 minutes
Cook time 10 minutes

· MY SECRET ·
To get these even crispier,
try Japanese-style panko
breadcrumbs. They feel
like toast and are amazing
with this recipe. Find them
in the Asian aisle at the
supermarket or at an
Asian shop.

2 garlic cloves, peeled
2 tbsp pine nuts
1 tbsp basil leaves
1 tbsp freshly grated Parmesan
 cheese
1 tsp peeled and roughly chopped
 fresh root ginger
1 red chilli, deseeded if you wish
$\frac{1}{2}$ tsp cumin seeds, toasted
 (see page 171) (optional)
juice of $\frac{1}{2}$ lemon
1 pack paneer, around 200g (7oz)
1 small naan bread – any flavour,
 but I like garlic and coriander
1 egg, beaten
2 tbsp vegetable oil or light olive oil

Tomato chutney
3 large tomatoes or 20 cherry
 tomatoes, roughly chopped
$\frac{1}{2}$ red onion, finely chopped
good pinch of kalonji (black onion
 or nigella) seeds (optional)
15 fresh curry leaves
 (see My Secret, page 20)
 (optional)
good pinch of dried chilli flakes
 or chilli powder
1 tbsp light brown sugar
1 tsp red wine vinegar
good pinch of salt, or to taste

Stuffed paneer bites

These are a wonderful snack to
have when you fancy something
a little naughty. I'm not a big
fan of paneer, which is the cheese
most commonly used in Indian
dishes, but when it's fried, all
that changes. It doesn't melt like
other cheese but rather softens,
and due to its neutral flavour it
makes it one of the most versatile
ingredients around. Here I have
made a stuffing quite similar
to a pimped-up pesto and then
rolled it in breadcrumbs, which
I make from slightly stale naan
bread but you can use ordinary
white bread instead. It tastes
best when served with a chutney,
so try this simple fresh tomato
one if you have time.

Gently heat all the tomato chutney ingredients together in a
saucepan for 10 minutes. Add a splash of water if it starts to
dry out, but allow it to thicken.

In the meantime, prepare the paneer bites. Make the stuffing for
the paneer by using a food processor to finely chop together the
garlic, pine nuts, basil, Parmesan, ginger, chilli and cumin with
the lemon juice (or chop very finely with a knife and mix together).
Give it a taste and adjust the seasoning if you think it needs it.

Cut the paneer in half as if you are about to make a sandwich.
Spread the stuffing on top of one layer and put the other paneer
layer on top. Cut it into large bite-sized pieces.

Make the breadcrumbs by pulsing the naan in the food processor,
or grate on a cheese grater, and put into a bowl.

Dip the paneer bites into the beaten egg in a bowl and then into
the breadcrumbs. Gently heat the oil in a large frying pan and fry
the paneer bites for a minute or so on each side until light golden
brown and crispy. Drain on kitchen paper. Serve them piled high
with the tomato chutney.

SERVES 4 AS A SNACK
Prep time 5 minutes
Cook time 20 minutes

300g (10^1/$_2$oz) unsalted mixed nuts
1 egg white, beaten until frothy
4 tbsp light brown sugar
1 tsp smoked paprika
1 tsp ground cinnamon

1–2 tsp chilli powder
2 tsp salt – I love sea salt
20 fresh curry leaves
   (see My Secret, page 20)
   (optional)

Bombay nuts

Nuts are the ultimate snack and even more so when dusted with spices, sugar and salt. Serve these at your next party and you'll be hearing praises all night! Sweet, salty, hot and smoky... the best combo.

Preheat the oven to 160°C/325°F/Gas Mark 3 and cover a large baking sheet with nonstick baking paper.

Mix the nuts with the egg white in a bowl and make sure the nuts are all coated well.

In a separate small bowl, stir together the sugar, spices and salt, then sprinkle over the nuts. Add the curry leaves (if using) and toss together before transferring the nuts to the lined baking sheet. Spread them out in a single layer.

Bake in the oven for 20 minutes, stirring them halfway through. Leave to cool on the baking sheet before breaking them apart and serving. They taste best warm.

SERVES 4
Prep time 10 minutes
Cook time 10 minutes

2 tbsp vegetable oil
1 cinnamon stick
1 tsp black mustard seeds
1 tsp ground turmeric
1/2 tsp black peppercorns,
    crushed with a pestle
    and mortar
20 fresh curry leaves
    (see My Secret, page 20)
    (optional)

2 spring onions, finely sliced
1 red chilli, finely sliced
1 tbsp peeled and julienned
    fresh root ginger
20 raw large tiger prawns,
    shells removed but tails
    left on, deveined
good pinch of salt
good drizzle of clear honey
2 tbsp roughly chopped
    fresh coriander

Tiger prawns with lime, ginger & mustard

Prawns are quick to cook and somehow feel rather exotic. This recipe borrows spices from the southern shores of India and I tasted a dish similar to this when I was learning about the local cuisine. My mouth was on fire with the chillies, but when I got past it I found the flavour to be delicate and delicious. I have toned down the chillies and added some background warmth by using fresh root ginger instead.

I'm using tiger prawns and I've removed most of the shell, apart from the tail. I prefer to leave the tail on, as it means that you have something to hold on to when biting into the prawns, but you can take the entire shell off if you prefer. Just make sure the prawns are raw and that they have been deveined.

Gently heat the oil in a large frying pan and add the cinnamon stick, mustard seeds, turmeric, peppercorns and curry leaves (if using). Once they start to sizzle, stir through the spring onions, chilli and ginger and allow to soften for around a minute.

Stir in the prawns and watch how they turn to a golden pink colour. Flip them over and sprinkle over a good pinch of salt. Once they are cooked through – and it won't take long, only a few minutes on each side – drizzle over the honey and sprinkle in half the coriander. Mix well and serve sprinkled with the remaining coriander.

Everyday spice box

Spices are the life and soul of all Indian dishes and are the ingredients that make your taste buds come to life. They brighten up even the simplest dishes by adding a little magic. As a little girl I would wander into the kitchen to see what wonderful dishes my family were creating as the scents wafted through the house. I came across my mum's spice box, which was the most amazing, colourful thing I'd ever seen. The smells were incredible but what surprised me most was the sheer amount she had crammed in there. As I grew up I learnt how to use these little potent wonders and I've been hooked ever since.

Each Indian family will fill their spice box with their favourite spices, some will even have two or three boxes depending how adventurously the family cooks. I like to keep one everyday box that contains most of the spices I need from all corners of India. I say 'most' because I can't quite fit every single spice from my pantry in there and if I want my dish to taste typically southern for example, then I need to add in a few extras. I have two layers to it – my base layer filled with tubs, and then the top layer packed with aromatic spices.

Buying super-fresh spices is a bit of an art, and something my father taught me. Spices have always been very special to him, not only as it was at the heart of our spice business, but he met my mum on one of his spice buying trips to India. Some spices are robust and don't lose much flavour as they age while others need to be bought as fresh as can be so they deliver the best possible flavour punch. Have you ever wondered why recipes taste different every time you cook them, even though you've made them the exact same way? It's down to the quality of your ingredients. If you hold onto spices for years, you will never have a fresh tasting dish as your core ingredients will have changed and lost their beautiful essence. I know buying fresh spices isn't always possible, not to mention affordable, so here are a few tips on how to buy and store my favourite spices that I keep in my everyday spice box.

Base layer spices

CORIANDER SEEDS

These seeds are one of the most important spices in my box. Coriander is one of the only spices that can be used throughout the recipe – seeds at the beginning, powder a little later on, and finished with the fresh leaf. I absolutely love the earthy lemony flavour it imparts in a dish and it is the perfect spice to create a good flavour base. The seeds can be toasted in a dry pan to help release their sweet flavour, and I like to sprinkle them on top of dishes to add a little mystery. Look for darkish beige-brown plump seeds. They turn light beige as they get older. Try with Tomato & Red Onion Salad with Roasted Coriander & Burrata (*see* page 84).

CUMIN SEEDS

I love love love cumin seeds. They help create a good flavour base, add a warm earthy note to dishes, and taste incredible when toasted and ground. Not to be confused with black cumin or royal cumin that add a very different flavour. Try and buy cumin seeds when they are brown, plump and unbroken. Try with Lentil Salad with Toasted Cumin Dressing or Cumin Roast Potatoes (*see* pages 96 and 146).

TURMERIC

A very special spice that doesn't seem to age. I call it the 'wonder' spice simply because it is truly wonderful. It has a unique healing ability that acts as a natural cleanser, drawing impurities out of everything it comes into contact with, which is why it is used to heal the body externally as well as internally. It's a member of the ginger family and looks slightly similar in appearance. It has an orangey yellow skin and is much smaller than root ginger, with bright orange flesh inside. If you can get your hands on fresh turmeric then you can pop it in the freezer, otherwise the more common form is dried and ground. Its yellow colour stains every single thing it touches and it can taste very bitter when raw, so I like to cook it well to bring out its slightly sweet flavour. Try with Scented Steamed Fish (*see* page 124).

BLACK PEPPER

Once known as the 'King of the Spices', it used to be one of the most expensive spices in the world and has a rich history. Unlike in the West where it is only used as a seasoning, Indian cooks use black pepper as a spice in its own right. Black pepper is surprisingly warm and brings a lot of heat to dishes. Buy dark black wrinkly peppercorns that are as whole as possible, they lose their flavour very quickly once ground. Try with Chilli Beef with Black Pepper (*see* page 60).

BLACK MUSTARD SEEDS

These tiny brown/black seeds add warmth and a slightly nutty flavour to dishes. They can be ground, made into a paste, used to flavour oil (mustard oil is very pungent), or used whole. They come in different sizes, and hold their flavour well as they age, so look out for dark-coloured seeds and whatever you do try not to drop the tub on the floor – they spread everywhere! Try with Wilted Mustard Greens (*see* page 158).

CHILLI POWDER

Chillies only gained fame in India a few centuries ago. Before that it was black pepper that was known for being the heat-infusing ingredient. Chilli powder can vary in heat level and it is only ever red as fresh green chillies can't be dried naturally. Bright deep-red chilli powder carries less heat and is made from Kashmiri red chillies, but the only way to tell how hot your chilli powder is, is to taste it! Made from dried red chillies, you can use the dried seeds inside to add more heat, or leave them out if you want a milder chilli powder. Try with Flaky Mint & Chilli Paratha (*see* page 149).

GARAM MASALA

The myth with garam masala is that it can only ever be one recipe. In truth, each cook will have his or her own recipe for garam masala, and may even have several masalas as each one works best with different dishes. Usually passed down from mother to daughter, my garam masala recipe was given to me by my mum and it is very precious to me. You can buy good garam masalas off the shelf, but there is nothing like making it fresh as ground masalas lose their potency quickly. Lightly toast whole spices (never turmeric) until fragrant and warm before tipping into a spice grinder. It can be a blend of anything from two spices up to 50 spices, whatever the cook wants it to be. Try with Crunchy Roast Cauliflower & Broccoli (*see* page 145).

Top layer spices

INDIAN BAY LEAVES

Indian bay leaves can't be substituted for European bay leaves as they have a different flavour, so leave them out if you don't have dried Indian bay leaves. If you're unsure what type yours are simply rub the leaves with your fingertips – if you can smell a hint of cinnamon then they are fine to use. Avoid buying leaves that are discoloured and holey. Try with One-pot Chicken with Smoked Spices (*see* page 46).

CINNAMON BARK

I love cinnamon and prefer to buy the bark as I can seek it out during cooking should I need to remove it. Its sweet mesmerizing flavour is best when whole and is lost quickly once ground into a fine powder. Try with Tadka Dhal (*see* page 154).

GREEN CARDAMOM

If black pepper is the 'King of the Spices' then this is its queen. Buy bright dark-green pods that aren't too shrivelled as the black seeds inside hold all the flavour. Green cardamom has a sweet camphor almost aniseed flavour and is by far my favourite spice. My first spice buying trip to India led me to a cardamom auction and I fell in love with this beautiful spice. Try with Roast Hazelnut & Cardamom Ice Cream (*see* page 176).

BLACK CARDAMOM

Although part of the same family as green cardamom, black cardamom is twice the size and more wrinkly, with a smoky aroma from being toasted on hot embers. Look out for large black dried pods that smell very smoky. Try with Black Dhal (*see* page 140).

MACE

This is the outer red lacy casing wrapped around fresh nutmeg. Mace turns orangey once dried and tastes almost perfumey with a gentle floral backnote. Look for whole pieces of mace that smell floral. Try with Foolproof Pilau Rice (*see* page 148).

CLOVES

Cloves have a medicinal flavour and cause a distinctive numbing sensation if chewed. You can tell they are fresh when they look plump and are a deep dark brown and almost black. The round heads should still be attached to their long stems and they should smell very strong. Try with Roast Stone Fruit & Honey with Pistachio Cream (*see* page 194).

STAR ANISE
This spice originally came from China but is now used in so many other cuisines across the world. It is by far the prettiest spice but its strong anise flavour can overpower a recipe so don't go too crazy. Look for large stars that have their pods still nestled in between the points. Try with Pineapple Anise Colada (*see* page 209).

SAFFRON
Although I don't keep saffron in my spice box, I do keep it in its very own special tub next to my box. Saffron strands are the stigmas of a variety of crocus flowers that only open for a few weeks of the year. Each flower produces only 3 stigmas and they have to be handpicked at dawn before the suns rays burn them. It is the world's most expensive spice and has a unique and enchanting floral flavour and colour. It's hard to know the quality of saffron without touching it and smelling it. Usually the more expensive it is, the

better quality it will be. Try with Saffron & Honey Naan Breads or Saffron, Cardamom & Thyme Celeriac (*see* pages 156 and 158).

Storing & using your spices

Always keep your spices in an airtight container. A spice box is perfect. Oxygen and sunlight age your spices quickly so try and keep them somewhere dark. When you grind spices to create powders you start to release their essential oils, their essence, which will then float off into the air as time goes on. Grinding your spices only as you need them will give you the best flavour so try and buy your spices whole and use them up quickly.

CHAPTER

2

BIG BITES

SERVES 6–8
Prep time 30 minutes
Cook time 5 hours

1 leg of lamb, about 2kg (4lb 8oz)
5 garlic cloves, peeled, 2 for the
  Spice Paste
4 rosemary sprigs, cut into
  small pieces
2 tbsp mint leaves
1 red chilli, deseeded if you
  wish, sliced
2 onions, finely sliced
500ml (18fl oz) hot lamb or
  vegetable stock or water
sea salt and pepper

Spice paste
1 tsp coriander seeds
2 tsp cumin seeds
2 tsp fennel seeds
1/2 tsp black peppercorns
1 tsp ground turmeric
2 tsp English mustard
4 tbsp vegetable oil

Slow-roast spiced lamb

Another Sunday lunch favourite in my home when I was growing up, this recipe is one I cook regularly when I have friends coming round. Making a simple spice paste to rub over the lamb infuses the meat while it roasts, and just in case there isn't enough flavour going on, I stud the lamb with herbs and garlic. The juices that sit in the roasting tray are perfect for gravy, which I prefer thin and unadulterated, but you can add some flour to thicken it if you prefer.

Low and slow is what makes the meat meltingly tender. It will taste even better if you can roast it at a lower temperature. For every 10°C/25°F/Gas Mark lower, add on an extra hour of cooking time. By the time it's ready, you won't even need a knife.

Preheat the oven to 140°C/275°F/Gas Mark 1. Make some deep cuts into the meat at evenly spaced intervals and poke a finger in the cuts to check that they are wide enough for the herbs and spices.

Make the spice paste by bashing up the coriander, cumin and fennel seeds with the peppercorns and 2 of the garlic cloves in a mortar with a pestle. Stir in the turmeric, mustard and oil, and mix well.

Slice the remaining garlic cloves ready for stuffing into the holes in the lamb. Rub the spice paste all over the lamb, making sure you get some into the holes. Fill the holes with the rosemary, mint, chilli and sliced garlic.

Toss the onions into a deep roasting tray, one that will fit the lamb snugly. Season the lamb well with salt and place on top. Pour in the hot stock or water, cover with foil and slow roast in the oven for 5 hours. Baste every hour with the spiced stock.

Remove from the oven and carefully place the lamb on a plate, cover with foil and leave to rest. The meat should be falling off the bone. Transfer the spiced stock to a saucepan (this is your gravy) and skim off any fat. Boil until reduced and thickened to your liking. Taste and adjust the seasoning with salt and pepper before serving with your slow-roast spiced lamb and maybe some Glazed Baby Potatoes (see page 116).

SERVES 4
Prep time 10 minutes
Cook time 1 hour

2 tbsp olive oil
3 bay leaves
2 cinnamon sticks
2 onions, finely sliced
100g (3½oz) pancetta or smoked
  bacon, cut into small pieces
2 portobello mushrooms,
  trimmed and sliced
3 garlic cloves, finely sliced
4 chillies, 2 sliced and 2 stabbed
  with a knife

8 chicken joints – a mix of thighs
  and drumsticks
400g (14oz) can chopped tomatoes,
  or 400g (14oz) fresh tomatoes,
  chopped
1 litre (1¾ pints) chicken stock
200g (7oz) new potatoes, cut in half
2 tbsp smoked paprika
1 tbsp garam masala
small bunch of fresh coriander

One-pot chicken with smoked spices

One-pot cooking is my ideal style of cooking – hardly any washing up and it usually doesn't involve too much effort. This is one of my dinner party favourites. After the chopping is done and you've started getting the flavours going, you simply move it to the oven and let it cook slowly. If anyone turns up late, then the chicken can sit happily bubbling away until you need it. Now that's what I call relaxed entertaining.

Preheat the oven to 180°C/350°F/Gas Mark 4.

Gently heat the oil in a large flameproof casserole dish, or other large pan that can go in the oven, and add the bay leaves and cinnamon sticks. After a minute, add the onions and allow to soften for 5 minutes. Stir in the pancetta or bacon and cook for 5 minutes until crispy, and the onions are golden brown. Stir in the mushrooms, garlic and chillies and allow to cook for 1 minute.

Add the chicken pieces, skin-side down, trying to fit them all in a single layer, as you want to crisp up the skin for a few minutes. Once the skin is golden brown, turn the chicken over and pour in the tomatoes, stock, potatoes, smoked paprika and garam masala. Cut the stalks off the coriander and finely chop them. Add the chopped stalks to the pan and give everything a good stir. Cover the pan with a lid (or with foil if you haven't got one) and transfer to the oven to finish cooking through. The chicken will be ready after 40 minutes.

Carefully remove the lid and push the chicken to the surface so that the skin is above the tomato sauce. Turn the oven to grill if it has that function, or transfer to a preheated high grill, and grill for a few minutes to allow the skin to turn crispy. In the meantime, roughly chop the coriander leaves. Sprinkle over before serving with some Wilted Mustard Greens (*see* page 158).

· MY SECRET ·
For a vegetarian version, add 500g (1lb 2oz) soaked, cooked and drained (or drained canned) chickpeas instead of chicken, leave out the bacon and use veggie not chicken stock. It tastes delicious.

SERVES 4
Prep time 15 minutes
Cook time 12 minutes

100g (3¹/₂oz) white long-grain
  rice – I like basmati
50g (1³/₄oz) light brown sugar
50g (1³/₄oz) English breakfast
  tea leaves
2 cinnamon sticks
2 tsp fennel seeds
8 cloves
1 tsp ground green cardamom
8 skin-on sea bass fillets,
  scaled and pin-boned

Marinade
2 tsp fennel seeds
3 garlic cloves, peeled
1 tbsp peeled and roughly
  chopped fresh root ginger
1–2 dried red chillies
3 tbsp roughly chopped
  fresh coriander
juice of 1 lemon or lime
2 tsp clear honey
good pinch of salt, or to taste

Chai-smoked bass

Steaming fish using tea leaves is an old Chinese tradition, so I've borrowed the technique and added some of my favourite chai spices to the leaves during smoking. You need to add sugar to the leaves to help the tea smoke, and the rice keeps the tea burning for longer. I'm using sea bass fillets here, with all the bones removed to make it easier to eat, but you can use whole fish instead – just make sure they've been well cleaned and gutted and their scales have been removed.

You need plenty of foil for this recipe and I like to put my fish on nonstick baking paper so that the skin doesn't stick. I'm using loose English breakfast tea, but you can always snip the top off a few tea bags and empty out the leaves.

Mix the rice, sugar and tea leaves together. Make the chai spice mix by roughly crushing the cinnamon sticks, fennel seeds and cloves using a pestle and mortar – they will release more flavour if they are broken up. Add them to the rice mixture and stir in the cardamom.

Line a large, heavy-based saucepan, or large, heavy roasting tray, with 2 sheets of foil. Toss the rice mixture onto the foil and spread evenly over the base. Cover loosely with another piece of foil, making sure some smoke can escape, and place the steamer, or rack, on top. Cover with a lid, or foil, place the pan or tray on the hob and turn on the heat to medium. Prepare the fish while you get the smoke going.

For the marinade, crush the fennel seeds with the pestle and mortar. Add the garlic, ginger, chillies and coriander, and bash together. Mix in the lemon or lime juice, honey and a good pinch of salt. Rub the marinade all over the fish fillets (or inside and out if using whole fish).

Lay 4 fish fillets, skin-side down, on a piece of nonstick baking paper and top with the other 4 fillets, skin-side up. Now you're ready to smoke the fish. Carefully lift the lid off the pan, or foil off the tray – it should have started to smoke by now – and place the fish on the paper on top of the steamer or rack. Put the lid, or foil, back on and cook for around 10–12 minutes (or, if using an ovenproof pan, place in an oven preheated to 200°C/400°F/Gas Mark 6). If you see smoke escaping, fit some foil tightly on to the rim of the pan.

Once cooked, remove the fish from the steamer, or rack, and serve with a lightly dressed salad.

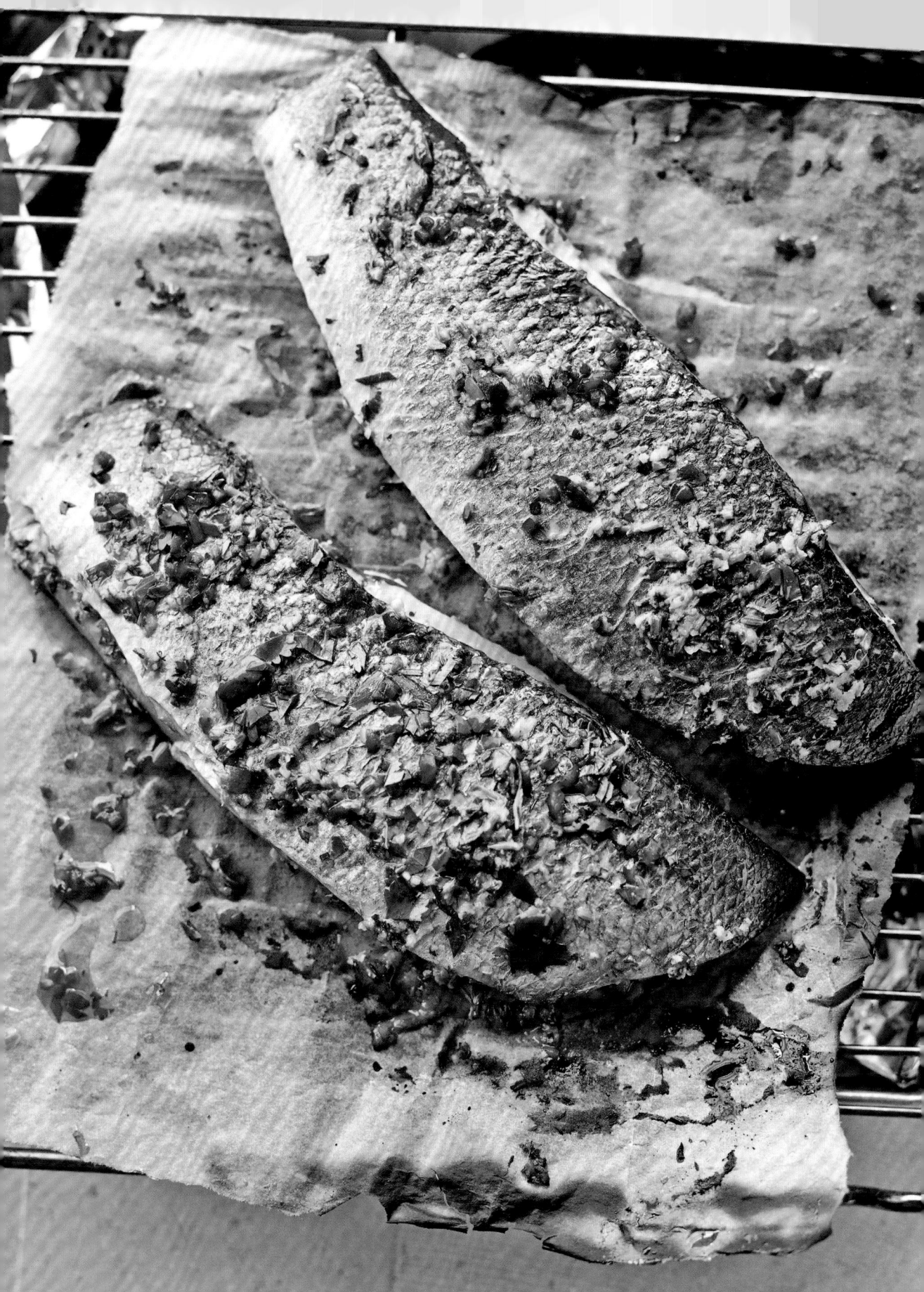

SERVES 4
Prep time 10 minutes
Cook time 40 minutes

4 steaks, about 200g (7oz) each –
use any cut you prefer but make
sure they are around 4cm (1¹/₂in)
thick and at room temperature
a few rosemary sprigs

Wedges
4 large baking potatoes, about 800g
(1lb 12oz), cut into wedges
2 tbsp light olive oil
2 tsp ground cumin
1 tsp smoked paprika

good pinch of sea salt and pepper
1 garlic bulb, cut in half horizontally

Steak marinade
2 tsp cumin seeds
¹/₄ tsp black peppercorns
¹/₂ tsp dried chilli flakes
1 tsp ground turmeric
2 garlic cloves, peeled
3 tbsp light olive oil
good pinch of sea salt

· MY SECRET ·
To cook the perfect steak,
make sure your pan is really hot
and don't add any oil. Oil your meat
instead with the spice marinade,
and try to get a good 'bark' (those
charred bits) before flipping it over.
It will add bags of flavour. Make
sure you allow your meat to rest
before cutting into it.

Sizzling steak & cumin paprika wedges

There is nothing quite like tucking into a perfectly cooked steak with some fluffy crispy fries on the side, or wedges in this case. This is a wonderful recipe for those days when you want an easy meal with little cooking. Adding some spice to your steak gives it a different dimension and it means you don't need to make a sauce – all you need is a little horseradish and maybe some ketchup for dunking the wedges.

I can't stress enough how important the quality of the meat is, so buy the best you can. And if you're a garlic lover, then definitely roast the entire bulb with the wedges. Keep the skins on and cut it through the middle horizontally so that the cloves are exposed. They will be sticky and sweet after roasting and taste incredible with the steak.

Preheat the oven to 200°C/400°F/Gas Mark 6. Mix all the ingredients for the wedges except the garlic together in a roasting tray, then add the garlic bulb halves, cut-side down, and roast in the oven for 40 minutes, or until the wedges are tender, crispy and golden brown. Give them a stir halfway through.

In the meantime, make the marinade for the steak. Gently heat a small frying pan and toast the cumin seeds, peppercorns and chilli flakes together for a few minutes until they are fragrant and the seeds are golden brown. Transfer to a mortar and allow to cool for a few minutes before grinding them with a pestle. Add the turmeric and garlic and pound to a paste. Pour in the oil and add a really good pinch of salt. Rub the marinade over the steaks and the sprigs of rosemary.

Heat a griddle pan until very hot. Chargrill the steaks on one side for a few minutes before flipping over and cooking on the other side. Using the coated rosemary sprigs, brush extra marinade over the steaks as they cook to layer up the flavour. Cook the steaks to your liking (and it all depends on what sort you are cooking) before removing and setting aside to rest for a few minutes. This allows all the juices to run back into the meat and keep it juicy.

Serve the steaks with the spicy wedges and the sweet roasted garlic.

SERVES 4
Prep time 15 minutes, plus
(preferably) marinating
Cook time 30 minutes

6–8 boneless chicken thighs,
skin removed and cut into
finger-length pieces

Tikka paste
2 tbsp natural yogurt
1 tsp ground turmeric
1/2 tsp chilli powder
1 tsp garlic paste
1 tsp ginger paste

Masala sauce
2 tbsp vegetable oil
4 green cardamom pods
1 cinnamon stick
1 tsp cumin seeds
1 large onion, finely sliced
2 tsp garlic paste

1 tsp ginger paste
3 green chillies, 1 finely sliced
and 2 stabbed with a knife
2 tbsp garam masala
1 tbsp ground coriander
2 tsp ground cumin
400g (14oz) can chopped
tomatoes, or 400g (14oz)
fresh tomatoes, chopped
15g (1/2oz) butter (optional)
6 tbsp double cream or
natural yogurt
good pinch of salt, or to taste
sugar, to taste
lemon juice, to taste
fresh coriander, to garnish

Chicken tikka masala

I couldn't not include a recipe for what has become the most famous Indian dish worldwide. Its story of origin varies. I was told this one…

An English army officer returning home from active duty visited his local Indian restaurant (and there weren't many around at the time). He demanded sauce with his chicken tikka, so the dutiful waiter trundled off to the kitchen to get some. The chef was fuming – tikka is always a dry dish – but to keep his customer happy he made a simple sauce from tomatoes and spices. He poured it over the chicken and, hey presto, chicken tikka masala was born!

Pouring sauce over the cooked chicken rather than allowing raw chicken to cook in the sauce is what has made this dish the most scrutinized in Indian culinary history.

Mix the tikka paste ingredients together in a bowl, add the chicken and turn to coat well. If you have time, cover and leave to marinate in the fridge overnight.

Start making the masala by gently heating the oil in a saucepan. Add the cardamom pods and cinnamon stick and wait for the cardamoms to begin turning white. Add the cumin seeds and when sizzling add the onion. Cook the onion for 5 minutes so that it turns translucent and starts to colour a little around the edges. Stir in the garlic, ginger and chillies. While you leave them to soften for a minute, mix the garam masala, ground coriander and cumin with a few tablespoons of water. Add to the pan and stir well. After a minute, stir through the tomatoes and butter (if using). Pour in 200ml (7fl oz) of water and leave the masala to simmer for about 15 minutes.

In the meantime, heat a griddle pan over a medium heat, or preheat the grill to medium, and cook the chicken tikka for about 10 minutes, turning often, or until cooked through.

Finish the masala sauce by stirring in the cream or yogurt (to make it lighter). Taste and adjust the flavours with salt, sugar and lemon juice if you need to.

You can either add the chicken tikka to the sauce or pour the sauce over the chicken for a truly authentic chicken tikka masala. Don't forget to scatter over fresh coriander right at the end.

SERVES 6–8
Prep time 10 minutes
Cook time about 4¹/₂ hours,
plus resting

1 tbsp sea salt
1 tbsp fennel seeds
1 boneless pork shoulder, about
    1.5–2kg (3lb 5oz–4lb 8oz), fat
    scored – your butcher can do
    this for you
2 onions, sliced
2 cinnamon sticks
2 bay leaves
1 red chilli, sliced
500ml (18fl oz) orange juice
100ml (3¹/₂fl oz) pomegranate
    molasses

50ml (2fl oz) tamarind paste/
    concentrate
50ml (2fl oz) white wine vinegar
2 tbsp clear honey
2 tbsp peeled and finely chopped
    fresh root ginger
1 tbsp chipotle chilli paste
2 tsp English mustard
good pinch of salt
seeds of 1 pomegranate

Slow-cooked tamarind-glazed pork

Slow cooking is one of the surest ways to seal in moisture and keep meat succulent and tender. This recipe of pork shoulder cooked low and slow, glazed with sweetly sour tamarind and pomegranate molasses, is certain to impress. There is enough fat in this cut of meat to keep the pork juicy, but I like to baste the meat often to really layer up those deeply intense flavours. Once the crackling is crispy, turn down the oven and cook the pork slowly until it falls apart.

Preheat the oven to 240°C/475°F/Gas Mark 9.

Grind the salt and fennel seeds together with a pestle and mortar. Rub it all over the pork, making sure you really get it into the cuts. Lay the onions, cinnamon sticks, bay leaves and chilli in the base of a roasting tray (one that fits the pork snugly) and place the pork on top, skin-side up. Pop in the oven for about 30 minutes, or until the crackling is golden brown and hard to the touch.

In the meantime, mix all the remaining ingredients except the pomegranate seeds together.

Once the crackling is ready, reduce the oven to 140°C/275°F/Gas Mark 1 and pour the orange juice mixture over the onions. Baste a little on to the flesh of the pork (not the crackling, or it will burn) and cook, uncovered, for about 4 hours, basting the meat every now and again. If you want to cook it for longer, then lower the heat. I suggest for every 10°C/25°F/Gas Mark lower you go, add on an extra hour of cooking time. The longer you cook it, the better it will be.

Take the pork out of the oven and baste one more time, including the crackling this time, then cover loosely with foil and leave to rest for around 20 minutes. The sauce in the roasting tray is going to be the gravy, so make sure you skim off any fat that rises to the top. If you prefer, you can pour the sauce into a saucepan and heat on the hob until thickened.

Sprinkle the pomegranate seeds over the pork and serve with lots of the gravy and the usual trimmings of roasties and greens.

· MY SECRET ·
For perfect crackling –
and let's be honest, that's
the best bit – use kitchen
paper to dry off the skin so
that it is bone dry before you
rub the salt and fennel mix
deep into the cuts.

SERVES 4
Prep time 20 minutes
Cook time 1 hour

Roasted vegetables
400g (14oz) mixed vegetables –
I like broccoli, peppers, carrots
and cauliflower – cut into large
bite-sized pieces
2 red onions, sliced
2 tbsp olive oil
1 tsp cumin seeds
2 tsp garam masala
1 tsp coriander seeds, roughly
crushed with a pestle and mortar
¼ tsp black peppercorns, roughly
crushed with a pestle and mortar
1 tsp ground turmeric
a few thyme sprigs

Rice
250g (9oz) white basmati rice
1 litre (1¾ pints) vegetable stock
1 tsp garam masala
4 cloves
4 green cardamom pods
2 cinnamon sticks
good pinch of saffron threads
(optional)
small handful of peas
1 tbsp peeled and julienned
fresh root ginger
1–2 red chillies, sliced
3 tbsp roughly chopped
fresh coriander

Roasted vegetable biryani

I visited India in search of the most outstanding biryani and I was lucky enough to track down the two regions that do it the best – Hyderabad and Lucknow. Both very different and both absolutely delicious. This is an ideal dish to make using leftovers; in fact, it tastes even better if you do. I know the ingredients list looks extensive, but there are two parts to the dish – the roasted vegetables and then the rice – and both need to be packed with flavour. So don't be put off trying out this sensational recipe. This biryani differs from the chicken one on page 62, as it is not layered.

Preheat the oven to 200°C/400°F/Gas Mark 6 while you prepare the veg for roasting. Lay them all, including the onion, in a large roasting tray and pour over the oil. Sprinkle over the spices and the thyme. Mix together well and then roast in the oven for 40 minutes.

In the meantime, get the rice ready. Wash it in several changes of water and leave to soak in cold water for around 30 minutes. This will soften the grains so that they cook more quickly, and also allow the beautiful flavour and fragrance to be released.

Drain the water off the rice. Pour the rest of the rice ingredients into a saucepan and bring to the boil. Stir in the rice and allow to cook uncovered for 7 minutes. Check that the grains are soft before draining off the stock, keeping a few tablespoons aside.

Take the roasted vegetables out of the oven, mix in the rice and pour over the reserved stock. Cover tightly with foil and pop back in the oven for a further 15 minutes.

Serve with lots of cooling Cucumber Raita made with mint (see page 166) and your favourite pickles and chutneys.

SERVES 4
Prep time 10 minutes
Cook time 10–15 minutes

naan breads
toppings of your choice (*see below*)

Naazas

Naazas are Indian pizzas using naan bread as a base. I came across this idea when I was developing recipes for my family business. We had so many extra naan breads floating around work and it was the perfect way to use them up. There are a million and one ways to top a pizza, so be experimental and see what you can come up with. I have split my favourite combos into sections to enable you to pick and choose whatever takes your fancy on the day. You can buy extra-large giant naans or mini ones.

Preheat the oven and a baking sheet (or pizza stone if you have one) to 220°C/425°F/Gas Mark 7.

Lay out the naan breads and spread with your choice of pizza sauce. Add your cheese or cheeses and your toppings and bake on the hot baking sheet (or pizza stone) for 10–15 minutes, or until the cheese has melted and is bubbling.

Pizza sauce bases

Passata mixed with chopped fresh coriander, chopped garlic, ground toasted cumin seeds (*see page 171*), a good pinch of chilli powder and salt and sugar to taste.

Mango Chutney (*see page 167*) (I know it sounds strange but it really works!) mixed with creamy blue cheese.

Sticky Sweet Date Chutney (*see page 168*) (another winner, I promise).

Kinda Indian pesto – blitz together toasted pine nuts, basil leaves, fresh coriander, freshly grated Parmesan cheese and red chilli in a food processor or blender, then drizzle in the tiniest glug of olive oil to bring it all together.

Cheeses

Try the usual Cheddar or mozzarella, or go for Brie, feta, goats' cheese or Gorgonzola – you can really mix it up here.

Toppings

Some of the standard favourites include mushrooms, peppers, olives and cured meats like salami – the list is endless.

Extra-special toppings

Sun-dried tomatoes, roasted peppers, artichokes, dried fruits such as raisins and dried cranberries, roasted nuts and exotic fruit like pomegranate seeds.

· **MY SECRET** ·
Some shop-bought naan breads can be rather stodgy and thick, so you may want to warm them up in the oven first to crisp them up a little and prevent your naazas going soggy. Or why not try making your own naan breads by following my recipe on page 156.

SERVES 4
Prep time 10 minutes
Cook time 45 minutes,
plus resting

1 can beer – any size or kind you like
1 tbsp peeled and roughly chopped
   fresh root ginger
grated rind of 1 lime, fruit halved
   for squeezing over
1 tsp coriander seeds
1 tsp cumin seeds
3 spring onions, roughly
   chopped
3 garlic cloves, roughly
   chopped

1 red chilli, roughly
   chopped
a few rosemary sprigs
1 tsp smoked paprika
1 tsp ground turmeric
2 tbsp vegetable oil – I like rapeseed
1.5kg (3lb 5oz) chicken,
   spatchcocked, legs slashed
   with a knife
sea salt and pepper

Drunken chicken

*The chicken isn't drunk,
it's just the way you cook it!
Cooking the bird over liquid,
I'm using beer, keeps the meat
moist and adds a little extra
flavour. I've added spices to
both the beer and the rub for
the chicken. That way the
chicken is subtly flavoured
inside and out and it's
absolutely delicious. Try
to get good quality meat as
it makes all the difference here.
If you spatchcock your chicken
you cut the cooking time in
half. It's easy to do yourself,
but you can always ask your
butcher to do this for you.*

Preheat the oven to 200°C/400°F/Gas Mark 6.

Pour the can of beer in a deep roasting tray and add the ginger,
lime rind and coriander seeds.

Make the rub for the bird. Using a food processor or pestle and
mortar, grind up the cumin seeds before adding the spring onions,
garlic, chilli and rosemary. Pulse or grind before stirring in the
smoked paprika, turmeric, oil and a really good pinch of salt and
pepper. Mix well to form a paste and rub it all over the chicken,
inside and out. There's no harm rubbing some under the skin, too.

Lay the chicken cut-side down on a rack that will fit over the
roasting tray awash with beer. Place the rack over the tray and cook
in the oven for 40 minutes (or longer if your chicken is larger) and
until the juices run clear. Turn the oven to grill if it has that function,
or transfer to a preheated medium grill. Allow the skin to crisp up
for 5 minutes. Rest the chicken for 10 minutes before serving with
a squeeze of lime and a crisp salad, such as Mixed Herb Salad
with Honey Pecan Dressing (*see* page 78).

· MY SECRET ·
Why not experiment
with different beers,
such as alcoholic ginger
beer or root beer to add
some extra flavour?

SERVES 4
Prep time 10 minutes
Cook time 10 minutes

2 tbsp vegetable oil
2 tsp black mustard seeds
$1/2$ tsp black peppercorns, finely
crushed with a pestle and mortar
1 cinnamon stick
15–20 fresh curry leaves
(*see* My Secret, page 20) – just leave
them out if you don't have fresh
1 tbsp peeled and julienned fresh
root ginger
2 tsp garlic paste, or pound 3 garlic
cloves with a pestle and mortar

3 green chillies, 1 sliced and 2 slit
down the middle but left whole
$1/2$ tsp ground turmeric
1 tbsp tomato purée, mixed with
2 tbsp water
600g (1lb 5oz) beef fillet, cut into
strips around 1cm ($1/2$in) thick
good pinch of salt, or to taste
good pinch of sugar, or to taste
finely sliced spring onions,
to garnish

Chilli beef with black pepper

*I first tasted an Indian dish that
was laced with chillies when I
was on a culinary trip around
coastal India a few years ago. It
was pretty fiery, but underneath
all that heat was a wonderful
warmth and flavour. This is
quite hot, so go easy on the
chillies if you can't handle
yours. I'm using the delicious,
tender cut of beef fillet, but you
can use any cut you like; just
make sure it's lean, otherwise it
will be chewy. It's pretty quick,
like a stir-fry, so try and use a
wok if you have one but if not
a large, heavy-based frying
pan will do. This is a great
recipe when you fancy
something big on flavour
but small on prep time.*

Gently heat the oil in a wok, or large heavy-based frying pan,
and add the mustard seeds, crushed peppercorns and cinnamon
stick. After a minute or so the mustard seeds will be jumping
out of the pan, so add the curry leaves, ginger, garlic, chillies
and turmeric. Allow to soften for a minute before pouring
in the tomato purée mix.

Stir well, then turn up the heat and add the beef. Keep moving
it around the pan so that it colours and then turns golden brown.
It will have more flavour if you allow it to caramelize, but be careful
not to burn the other ingredients. The beef won't take long to cook
– around a minute if you like it pink in the middle.

Taste and adjust the seasoning with salt and sugar. Sprinkle over
some sliced spring onions and serve with my simple Foolproof
Pilau Rice (*see* page 148) and a well-needed cooling Cucumber
Raita (*see* page 166).

· MY SECRET ·
Adding whole chillies,
as well as sliced, gives the
dish background warmth
instead of burning heat.
Pick them out and bite
into them if you fancy
a real heat kick!

SERVES 4
Prep time 20 minutes
Cook time 1 hour

Chicken
3 tbsp vegetable oil
2 large onions, finely sliced
2 tsp coriander seeds, roughly
  crushed with a pestle and mortar
1 tbsp peeled and finely chopped
  fresh root ginger
2 garlic cloves, finely chopped
1 red or green chilli, finely chopped
8 chicken joints, cut in half
  (*see* My Secret, opposite) – I like
  a mix of drumsticks and thighs
1^1/$_2$ tbsp garam masala
1 tbsp ground cumin
1 tsp ground turmeric
^{1}/$_2$ tsp chilli powder (optional)
good pinch of salt, or to taste
6 tbsp natural yogurt

Rice
300g (10^1/$_2$oz) white basmati rice
6 cloves
4 green cardamom pods
2 cinnamon sticks
2 bay leaves
good pinch of saffron threads
  (optional)
good pinch of salt, or to taste
1 tbsp peeled and julienned
  fresh root ginger, for layering
2 garlic cloves, finely chopped,
  for layering
1 chilli, finely chopped,
  for layering (optional)
3 tbsp roughly chopped
  fresh coriander

Chicken biryani

I always get asked what my last supper would be and this is high on my list. My partner grew up with some of the best biryanis in the world, as his family hail from Hyderabad, so I made sure I stepped up my game when I started cooking for him. This is one of his favourite meals and I hope it will become one of yours.

This is a layered biryani, which means that you cook the chicken separately and then layer it with fragrant cooked rice. I don't usually like recipes that have an ingredients list as long as your arm, but sadly this one is quite long. Trust me, it's totally worth it!

Preheat the oven to 200°C/400°F/Gas Mark 6.

First, start the chicken. Gently heat half the oil in a large saucepan and cook the onions for around 10 minutes until they are light golden brown and catching around the edges. Take half out and set aside, keeping the other half frying until they are crispy – these are for layering. Take these crispy onions out and set aside for later.

Pour the remaining oil into the pan and return the first set of soft golden brown onions with the coriander seeds. Once they are sizzling, add the ginger, garlic and fresh chilli. Cook for a further minute before adding the chicken, garam masala, cumin, turmeric, chilli powder and enough water to come three-quarters of the way up the chicken (about 350ml/12fl oz should be fine). Add a good pinch of salt, cover and leave the chicken to cook for 20 minutes.

In the meantime, get the rice ready. Wash it in several changes of water and leave to soak in cold water for around 10 minutes. This will soften the grains so that they cook more quickly, and also allow the beautiful flavour and fragrance to be released.

Drain the water off the rice. Fill a saucepan with boiling water and stir in the cloves, cardamom pods, cinnamon sticks, bay leaves and saffron (if using). Add a good pinch of salt, stir and add the rice. Allow to cook uncovered for about 7 minutes, or until the grains are almost cooked through. Drain off the excess water and set aside while you finish the chicken.

Remove the chicken from the sauce and set aside. Turn off the heat and stir the yogurt into the sauce, which will thicken it. Now it's time to layer up the biryani.

In an ovenproof dish (I like to use a clear one so that you can see all the layers), start with a layer of rice. Then add some chicken and cover with a little thickened sauce. Sprinkle over some ginger, garlic and chilli, followed by some of the reserved crispy onions and fresh coriander. Keep layering up the biryani, finishing with a final layer of rice sprinkled with the last of the crispy onions and fresh coriander, then tightly cover the dish with foil.

Pop in the oven for 15 minutes to steam and fuse the ingredients together. Serve with lots of cooling Cucumber Raita made with mint (*see* page 166) and your favourite pickles and chutneys.

· MY SECRET ·
This recipe works best if you use halved chicken joints, as it adds more flavour and they cook more quickly than whole joints, so ask your butcher to prepare them for you.

SERVES 4
Prep time 10 minutes
Cook time 20 minutes

2 tbsp vegetable oil, plus extra
  if needed
1 pack paneer, around 225g (8oz),
  cut into large bite-sized pieces
20 fresh curry leaves
  (*see* My Secret, page 20)
  (optional)
2 tsp black mustard seeds
1 tsp cumin seeds
1 tsp ground turmeric
1 onion, finely diced
2 garlic cloves, finely chopped
1 tbsp peeled and finely chopped
  fresh root ginger

2 red chillies, 1 finely sliced, 1 slit
  down the middle but left whole
2 tbsp tomato purée
1 tbsp garam masala
2 tsp ground coriander
400ml (14fl oz) coconut milk
100g (3½oz) broccoli florets
1 tbsp tamarind paste/concentrate,
  or to taste
salt
sugar, to taste
small handful of fresh coriander,
  to garnish

Paneer & broccoli masala

Making a masala from scratch is a lot easier than you think. I've made a few changes to a classic recipe that uses flavours from the shores of southern India. Frying the paneer in a little oil before stirring it through the masala not only makes it crispy but also adds bags of flavour.

Gently heat the oil in a saucepan and fry the paneer until it's golden brown on all sides. Remove from the pan and set aside for later.

Throw the curry leaves (if using) into the pan to crisp up. Take them out and reserve for sprinkling over at the end.

Add a little more oil to the pan if you need to and toss in the mustard and cumin seeds. Once they start sizzling, stir in the turmeric and onion. Allow to soften for a few minutes before stirring in the garlic, ginger and chillies. After a further minute, stir in the tomato purée, garam masala and ground coriander.

Add a splash of water to the pan and pour in the coconut milk. Bring to a simmer and toss in the broccoli and fried paneer. Stir through the tamarind and simmer for 5 minutes. Taste and adjust the seasoning with salt and sugar. Garnish with the crispy curry leaves and the fresh coriander before serving with some steamed basmati or my Foolproof Pilau Rice (*see* page 148) to mop up the sauce.

SERVES 4–6
Prep time 15 minutes
Cook time 40 minutes

1 whole skin-on salmon, about
  1kg (2lb 4oz), cleaned, boned
  and head removed
1 tbsp finely chopped garlic
1 tbsp peeled and finely chopped
  fresh root ginger
1–2 red chillies, sliced
2 tbsp natural yogurt
2 tsp black mustard seeds
1 tsp ground turmeric
1 tsp clear honey
good pinch of salt

200g (7oz) crunchy vegetables –
  I like celeriac, leeks and carrots
  – all julienned
20 fresh curry leaves
  (see My Secret, page 20)
  (optional)
1 tbsp desiccated coconut, toasted
  (see My Secret, page 182)
  (optional)
1 tbsp roughly chopped chives
1 tbsp roughly chopped dill
2 limes, cut into quarters

Whole roasted salmon

This is my take on an ancient Indian recipe of stuffing a whole fish with spices, sealing it in an earthenware pot, burying it in the ground and covering it with natural heat fermenters. I'm using an oven to replicate the heat and I've chosen to use a whole salmon, but you can easily use individual fillets if you like. This will soon become one of your show-stopper recipes that will wow all your guests.

Preheat the oven to 180°C/350°F/Gas Mark 4. In the meantime, make deep cuts through the skin of the salmon.

Make the marinade for the fish by bashing together the garlic, ginger and most of the chilli slices with a pestle and mortar. Mix in the yogurt, mustard seeds, turmeric, honey and a good pinch of salt. Rub the marinade all over the salmon, inside and out.

Stuff the salmon with the julienned vegetables and sprinkle in the curry leaves (if using), coconut, chives and dill. Line a large roasting tray with foil and lay the fish on top. Toss in the lime quarters and roast in the oven for 40 minutes. (If using individual fillets, roast for half the time.)

Carve the fish at the table and serve with Cucumber Raita made with mint (see page 166) and Cumin Roast Potatoes (see page 146).

Storecupboard must-haves

As well as my spice box (see pages 36–41) there are a few ingredients I always keep stocked up. You never know when you may need them, and if I don't have time to pop to the market I know I can still eat well with my storecupboard must-haves.

BASMATI RICE

There are so many varieties of rice to choose from but my favourite is basmati. Grown in northern India it has a delicate flavour and unique aroma. Some say you can smell the foothills of the Himalayas when cooking basmati and I have to agree. It's best washed in several changes of water to rinse off any starch, and then soaked for around half an hour to allow the grains to lengthen. This will improve the flavour of the rice and also reduce the cooking time as the grains will have softened. If you soak it for too long they will break during cooking and you will have bitty rice.

DHAL/LENTILS

Dhal/lentils last for ages and are bland, which means they carry flavour well – ideal for spice cooking. One of my favourite comfort dishes is Tadka Dhal (see page 154), which doesn't take long to make once the lentils are soft. With so many different varieties available you won't get bored. I like to boil more lentils than I need and pop them in the freezer. When I'm tired after a long day I just cover the frozen block in boiling water, throw in some flavours and I've got myself a fuss-free meal.

CHICKPEAS/CHANNA

You can boil them yourself but I keep the cooked tinned kind in my pantry. They taste great thrown into a salad, warmed with spices, or you can even mash them down and create a veggie burger.

CHICKPEA FLOUR/BESAN FLOUR/GRAM FLOUR

You would never make this yourself, although you could, but as it can be found at all good supermarkets you won't need to. Great for those intolerant to gluten, it has an almost nutty flavour once cooked and can be used to coat ingredients as well as thicken sauces.

TINNED TOMATOES

I think everyone should keep at least one tin of chopped tomatoes in their pantry, if they don't already. They are picked at their best so usually have a sweeter flavour than the store-bought tomatoes we are used to all year round. If I get great fresh tomatoes from a farmers' market I prefer to use them, otherwise I always have my tinned ones to fall back on.

TOMATO PURÉE

You will always find tomato purée in my pantry. I use it often, for those times I need to add a rich, intense tomato flavour to my dishes. I also like to use it as a background flavour to add warmth and sweetness to dishes, such as my Paneer & Broccoli Masala (*see* page 64).

TAMARIND

I prefer keeping the tamarind pulp (sometimes called concentrate) as all the hard work of removing the flesh from the seeds has been done for me. You can buy it in blocks that need soaking in warm water, or in a paste, which has a thick consistency and a strong concentrated flavour. You can even find whole tamarind, which look fab. Tamarind makes for fantastic chutneys (like my Sticky Sweet Date Chutney, *see* page 168) and adds a sweet-sour flavour to dishes such as my Slow-Cooked Tamarind-Glazed Pork (*see* page 54).

COCONUT MILK

I love to keep a few tins of coconut milk not only for savoury recipes but also for desserts. In India people will make or buy their coconut milk fresh, which is simply done by pressing the coconut flesh. Once the liquid has settled you can separate the milk that will contain some rich coconut cream, too. Some tinned brands of coconut milk contain more coconut cream than others, so I always store some coconut cream tins in case the coconut milk's not quite thick enough.

CHAPTER

FEEL-GOOD
FACTOR

SERVES 4
Prep time 5 minutes
Cook time 25 minutes

250g (9oz) quinoa, washed, and if necessary soaked and drained according to the packet instructions

enough vegetable stock to cook the quinoa according to the packet instructions (about 850ml/1^1/$_2$ pints)

1 tsp cumin seeds
1 tsp ground coriander
^{1}/$_2$ tsp ground ginger
1 large carrot, sliced into ribbons using a vegetable peeler

2 spring onions, finely sliced
8 sun-dried tomatoes in oil, drained and sliced
3 tbsp roughly chopped fresh coriander
2 tbsp olive oil
juice of 1 lime
sea salt and pepper
seeds of 1 pomegranate, to garnish (optional)
natural yogurt, to serve

Quinoa with carrot & lime

Quinoa is a seed that has become one of the most sought-after ingredients to add to your diet. Loved by vegans and those with a gluten allergy, it's packed with protein including all eight of the essential amino acids your body needs. Healthy or what?! It can be slightly bitter and therefore some varieties call for washing and soaking them first, so have a read of the packet instructions before cooking. You will have to boil it up for around 20 minutes and either wait for the liquid to be absorbed or drain it off. I like to use vegetable stock instead of plain boring water, and add some spices to give it a burst of life. I read that there are around 1,800 varieties of quinoa, so use whatever colour you prefer.

Cook the quinoa according to the packet instructions, using vegetable stock instead of water and stirring in the cumin seeds and ground coriander and ginger, until the stock has been absorbed and the quinoa is soft and plump.

You can either then leave the quinoa to cool before mixing in the remaining ingredients (except the pomegranate seeds and yogurt) or you can toss it all together while still hot. Taste and adjust the seasoning if you need to. Sprinkle over the pomegranate seeds (if using) to garnish and serve with some yogurt on the side.

· MY SECRET ·
You can use couscous instead of quinoa. I like the giant type. Cook according to the packet instructions in vegetable stock, adding the spices to the boiling hot stock. You may need to add a little more seasoning, as couscous doesn't have as much flavour as quinoa.

SERVES 4
Prep time 5 minutes
Cook time around 30 minutes

1 fennel bulb, trimmed and
thinly sliced
3 tbsp olive oil
1 tsp cumin seeds
$1/4$ tsp ground turmeric
4 garlic cloves, kept in their skins
300g ($10^1/2$oz) green beans
rind, pared in large pieces, and
juice of $1/2$ lemon

2 spring onions, finely sliced
1 red chilli, deseeded if you don't
like your salads fiery, finely sliced
200g (7oz) spinach leaves
2 tbsp roughly chopped mint leaves
salt
1 tbsp sesame seeds, toasted, to
sprinkle (optional)

Green bean salad with roasted fennel, garlic & mint

Fennel seed is a spice that often divides people, as it has a strong aniseed flavour. The fresh fennel bulb also has a very overpowering flavour, but when roasted it becomes sweet and mellow. I love adding spices before it's roasted to give some depth and then tossing it through greens while it's still warm for a pick-me-up salad.

Preheat the oven to 200°C/400°F/Gas Mark 6. Put the fennel slices in a roasting tray and drizzle over half the oil. Rub them with the cumin seeds and turmeric and then add the garlic cloves. Roast for 25 minutes until the fennel is lightly golden brown at the edges. Remove from the oven and allow to cool a little.

In the meantime, blanch the green beans by cooking them in a saucepan of boiling water with the lemon rind. Cook for 2 minutes before draining and plunging them into ice-cold water to keep their vibrant green colour. Discard the lemon rind.

Toss the green beans together with the spring onions, chilli, spinach and mint in a bowl.

When cool enough to handle, squeeze the roasted garlic cloves out of their skins and roughly chop them before adding them to the salad with the warm fennel. Drizzle over the remaining oil and lemon juice, then taste and season with salt accordingly, before serving sprinkled with the toasted sesame seeds, if you wish.

Bapuji (left) and Baa (back right) with their six children (including Dad – front) at Allcroft Road, London. Baa was clearly used to cooking in large batches with all those mouths to feed!

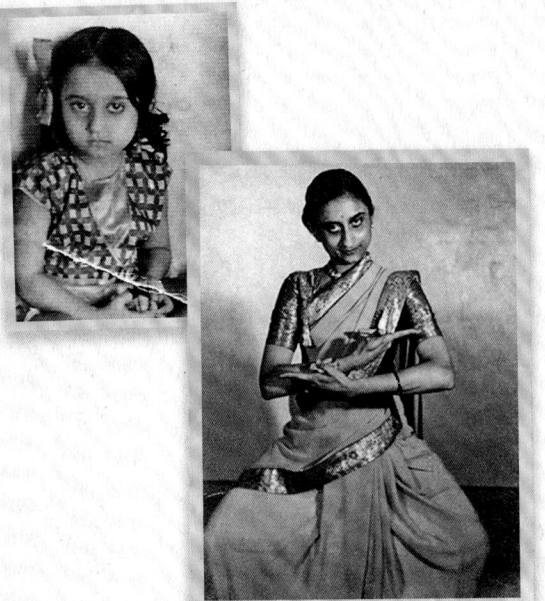

Mum's mother, Hansa, loved to dance. She was a dentist by profession but always found time to indulge in her favourite hobby.

Mum and her brother, Ajay
Uncle to me, with Tintin (right)
and dressed up for a family
get-together (below right).

Mum's father, Naishad, was
an officer in the Indian army.
This photo was taken when he
was young but he quickly rose
through the ranks and soon
became a colonel. Growing up
travelling to and from different
army bases meant that Mum
saw a lot of India from a very
young age.

200g (7oz) mixed salad leaves
1 large carrot, sliced into ribbons
using a vegetable peeler
1 red onion, finely sliced
50g (1³/₄oz) drained sun-dried
tomatoes in oil (oil reserved –
see right), roughly chopped
8 tbsp mixed herbs, roughly chopped
– I like a mix of fresh coriander,
mint, basil and parsley

2 tbsp oil – I like to use the oil from
the sun-dried tomatoes but
rapeseed oil or olive oil is fine
1 tbsp clear honey
2 tsp mustard – English or whatever
type you like
juice of 1 lemon, or to taste
good pinch of sea salt, or to taste
50g (1³/₄oz) pecan nut halves,
roughly chopped

Mixed herb salad with honey pecan dressing

*I love salads and am always
thinking of new ways to dress
them up. Sometimes I try out
different leaves, but usually
I play around with the
ingredients in my pantry to
see what dressings I can make.
This is a simple salad with a
trusty honey pecan dressing.*

Toss together the salad leaves, carrot, red onion, sun-dried
tomatoes and herbs.

Make the dressing by whisking all the remaining ingredients
together, adding the pecans once everything is combined.
Taste and add more salt or lemon juice if you need to.

Lightly dress the salad with the dressing before piling high
and tucking in.

· MY SECRET ·
For a little more crunch,
drench the pecans in honey
on a baking sheet and roast in a
preheated oven at 180°C/350°F/Gas
Mark 4 for 10 minutes while you
prepare the other ingredients.
Then toss through the salad.
Simply divine.

SERVES 4
Prep time 5 minutes
Cook time up to 30 minutes

500g (1lb 2oz) mixed-coloured
 raw beetroot, peeled and cut
 into wedges
2 tbsp rapeseed oil
1 tsp black mustard seeds
1 tsp ground ginger
50g (1³/₄oz) whole blanched
 hazelnuts
150g (5¹/₂oz) paneer, cut into
 large bite-sized pieces

2 tbsp natural yogurt
1 tbsp horseradish sauce
juice of ¹/₂ lemon
1 tbsp roughly chopped dill
good pinch of sea salt
drizzle of clear honey, to taste
100g (3¹/₂oz) watercress

Paneer & roasted beet salad

Paneer is a cows' milk cheese that has a texture similar to haloumi. Now I know that this is a recipe to make you feel good and so should be low in fat, but I have used paneer for a little indulgence. And I figured if I'm going to have the cheese, then I might as well cook it the way it tastes best, which is to pan-fry it so that the edges go slightly crispy. But you can leave it out altogether if you like. I always eat with my eyes, so I'm using different-coloured beets.

Preheat the oven to 200°C/400°F/Gas Mark 6. Put the beetroot in a roasting tray and drizzle over half the oil. Rub them with the mustard seeds and ginger and roast for 25 minutes. Add the hazelnuts and allow them to toast with the beets for 5 minutes.

In the meantime, gently heat up the remaining oil in a frying pan, add the pieces of paneer and pan-fry, moving them around often, until they are golden brown on all sides. Drain on kitchen paper while you make the dressing.

Whisk together the yogurt, horseradish, lemon juice, dill, salt and honey in a small bowl.

Remove the roasted beetroot and toasted hazelnuts from the oven, then toss with the pan-fried paneer, watercress and dressing.

SERVES 4
Prep time 5 minutes
Cook time 10–15 minutes

2 tbsp olive oil
1 tbsp tamarind concentrate/paste
1 tbsp clear honey
1 garlic clove, crushed
1 tsp cumin seeds, toasted (*see page 171*) and roughly crushed with a pestle and mortar
good pinch of salt, or to taste
good pinch of cracked black peppercorns

2 large aubergines, thinly sliced
1 large red chilli
1 red onion, finely sliced
200g (7oz) drained canned chickpeas
100g (3½oz) rocket leaves
juice of ½ lime
60g (2¼oz) feta cheese (optional)

Roast aubergine salad with chickpeas & tamarind

This is perfect to have when you fancy something good for you, but you definitely need something carby to bulk it out. Aubergines are one of the best ingredients to pair with spices, as they are like sponges and soak up any flavours you put with them. For this recipe I have made a marinade that doubles up as a dressing.

Preheat a griddle pan over a fairly high heat or, if baking in the oven, set it to 200°C/400°F/Gas Mark 6.

Make the marinade/dressing by mixing together the olive oil, tamarind, honey, garlic, cumin and the salt and cracked pepper.

Rub half the marinade on the aubergine slices and whole chilli, add to the hot griddle pan and cook for around 10 minutes, turning a couple of times, until soft. If cooking in the oven, spread out on a baking sheet and bake for around 15 minutes, turning once.

Once the aubergine is cooked, roughly chop the chilli. Toss the red onion, chickpeas and rocket with the lime juice and remaining dressing in a bowl. Gently mix in the aubergine and chopped chilli. Serve piled high, with some crumbly salty feta if you fancy it.

· MY SECRET ·
Tamarind is known as the date of India. If you don't have any, add some lime juice and dried fruit, such as dates, or pomegranate molasses to the dressing to give it a sweet–sour flavour.

SERVES 4
Prep time 5 minutes
Cook time 2 minutes

3 tbsp olive oil
1 tbsp coriander seeds
$1/4$ tsp black peppercorns, lightly crushed with a pestle and mortar
30 cherry tomatoes (mixed colours look great), halved or quartered depending on size, or 4 large tomatoes, thickly sliced

1 small red onion, finely sliced
good pinch of sea salt
2 tbsp basil leaves
good drizzle of balsamic vinegar
125g ($4^1/2$oz) burrata (or mozzarella)

Tomato & red onion salad with roasted coriander & burrata

One of my favourite chefs serves a dish similar to this at his restaurant in London. I have added some more spices to mine and combined it with the traditional tomato and red onion salad that I loved growing up. Burrata is similar to mozzarella but contains cream to make it richer. It tastes divine, so do seek it out for this recipe.

Gently heat the oil in a small frying pan and add the coriander seeds and peppercorns. As soon as they start sizzling, turn off the heat and allow them to scent the oil.

Delicately toss the tomatoes with the red onion in a bowl. Season with a good pinch of salt and spoon over half the toasted spices, including some of the scented oil. Toss to coat the ingredients evenly before sprinkling over the basil leaves and drizzling with balsamic vinegar.

Leaving the burrata whole, place with the salad and top with the remaining toasted spices. This is a real sharing salad, so rip open the burrata as you serve it.

1 shallot, finely chopped
1 tbsp peeled and finely chopped
    fresh root ginger
1–2 red chillies, deseeded if
    you don't like your salads
    with a chilli kick
1 tbsp palm sugar, or to taste,
    roughly chopped
juice of 1 lime
1 1/2 tbsp light or dark soy sauce,
    or to taste

2 tbsp toasted sesame oil
1 cucumber
15 radishes, trimmed and
    finely sliced
300g (10 1/2oz) mixed bean sprouts
    or mixed pea and bean sprouts
    (*see* My Secret, page 96)
3 tbsp roughly chopped mint, plus
    whole leaves to garnish (optional)
50g (1 3/4oz) salted peanuts,
    roughly crushed

Radish, peanut & mint salad

*I came across some amazing
salads when I visited Thailand
a few years ago to learn about
Thai cooking. When I got
home, the first thing I did was
stock up on all those essential
Thai ingredients and I've been
using them in my cooking
ever since. Here I've used palm
sugar to give my dressing a
little sweetness, but you can
use brown sugar if you don't
have any.*

Make the dressing by pounding the shallot, ginger and chillies with
a pestle and mortar. Add the palm sugar and pound again until it's
all dissolved. Stir in the lime juice, soy sauce and sesame oil. Taste
and add more soy sauce if you prefer it saltier, and palm sugar for
extra sweetness.

Slice the cucumber into ribbons using a vegetable peeler or really
thinly with a knife. Make sure you use the skin too, as this will add
a lovely colour and flavour to the salad. Stop when you reach the
watery core. Mix the cucumber ribbons with the radishes, sprouts
and most of both the mint and peanuts in a bowl.

Pour in the dressing and toss well to coat. Serve sprinkled with the
remaining mint and peanuts for the ultimate crunchy Asian salad.

· MY SECRET ·
This salad tastes best when
dressed just before you serve
it. You can make the dressing
beforehand and toss it
through the crunchy
salad at the last minute.

Magical chillies

Chillies are truly incredible. They come in all sorts of shapes and sizes and their heat levels vary considerably from pleasantly warm through to eye-wateringly hot. They are full of antioxidants, high in vitamin C that will help keep that cold at bay, and can help reduce cholesterol – they really are magical. When I was young you could only buy one type of mild chilli from the supermarket, and the fiery Indian finger chillies were only available from the Indian shop. Now you can buy all sorts of exotic varieties, each with its own unique flavour.

Each and every one of us has a different chilli tolerance and each chilli you buy or grow will never be the same as the last, which is why I always test every chilli before I add it to a recipe. Some people like to follow recipes exactly to the letter, and never improvise with the ingredient list. When cooking with spice and heat I think it's essential to change the recipe slightly.

If a recipe says three chillies, should you throw in three? Your chillies may be very different to the ones used by the chef who created it – worst of all – yours may be much hotter. Of course you can always snip the end off a chilli and have a nibble to check the heat, but it's pretty risky as it could blow your head off! I find it better to snip the end and then have a little smell. If it burns your nose, then it's likely to burn everything else. If you can't sense any heat, simply rub the cut end with your fingertip and tap the inside of your lip.

The general rule of thumb is the larger the chilli, the milder it is, but I have been caught out one too many times using this guide alone. It really is worth checking every chilli: you'll always get that one rogue that is either crazy hot or has no heat whatsoever.

The seeds and the white membrane inside the chilli carry most of the heat, which can easily be removed if you want to tone down a recipe. If doing this, save the seeds and dry them out. You can sow them and have a flourishing chilli plant in no time. Be patient: the white flowers bloom before you see any green chillies. You can pick them green and use them fresh or freeze them, or leave them on the plant to change to yellow, orange, red and sometimes even purple (only in very hot climates). Chillies taste sweeter as they ripen and the red ones dry the best. The ultimate question is which are hotter – green or red? If they are the same variety then they will be the same in heat, but ripe red chillies are sweeter than the under-ripe green ones.

If you want to add some extra flavour to your dishes as well as heat then try some of these chilli varieties:

JALAPEÑOS
They are around 7¹/₂cm (3in) long and usually eaten when green. They have a mild citrus flavour and are quite fiery.

CHIPOTLE
This is one of my favourite chillies. It's a smoked, dried jalapeño, which carries the same heat as a standard jalapeño but is slightly sweeter and has a beautiful smoky flavour. Try with Spicy Smoky Potatoes (see page 106).

FINGER CHILLIES
There are different types of finger chillies but I'm talking about the Indian ones. They are thin and as long as your finger (hence the name), and pretty hot even for my standards. Usually sold green, but if you grow your own you should try them when red, as they are delicious. Try using finger chillies in place of the whole chillies in Chilli Beef with Black Pepper and Black Dahl (see pages 60 and 140).

HABANERO
This is a really hot variety and usually used in Mexican cooking. You will see them when they are orange or red so buy what you can find and only use a little bit, I tend to use one to serve four people. The habanero has a tropical flavour and goes great in tomato dishes.

SCOTCH BONNET
One of the fieriest chillies around, these chillies are very VERY hot and they originate from the Caribbean. They are also known as 'Ball of Fire' because that's exactly what they are! Once you get past the heat you will see they have a fruity flavour that is rather nice.

CHAPTER

4

VEGGIES GALORE

SERVES 4
Prep time 10 minutes
Cook time 1 hour

2 butternut squash, cut in half lengthways and seeds removed
1 tsp cumin seeds
1/2 tsp coriander seeds
1/2 tsp black peppercorns
1/2 tsp dried chilli flakes
1 tsp garam masala
1 tbsp vegetable oil or light olive oil

50g (1³/₄oz) spinach leaves, roughly chopped
50g (1³/₄oz) feta cheese, crumbled
2 garlic cloves, finely chopped
2 tbsp finely chopped mint leaves
6 sun-dried tomatoes in oil, drained and roughly chopped
grated rind and juice of 1 lemon

Balti-baked squash with feta, tomato & mint

Baked butternut squash rubbed with balti spices and filled with salty feta, sweet sun-dried tomatoes and fresh mint. No wonder this is a great veggie dish that is filling and packs a lot of flavour.

There is no recipe as such for 'balti', as it actually refers to the pot that the dish is cooked in rather than a particular spice mix. However, across the world you can find balti spice blends and they typically contain the spices I have used in this recipe, so I have called this dish a balti in terms of the particular spicing of the dish.

Preheat the oven to 200°C/400°F/Gas Mark 6. Lay the squash, cut-side up, on a baking sheet.

Roughly crush the cumin and coriander seeds, peppercorns and chilli flakes with a pestle and mortar before mixing in the garam masala and oil. Rub all over the squash, especially on the flesh side, and bake in the oven for 45 minutes, or until you can put a knife through the flesh of the squash easily.

In the meantime, make the filling by mixing together the spinach, feta, garlic, mint, sun-dried tomatoes and lemon juice.

When the squash is soft, take out of the oven and scoop out nearly all the flesh, leaving a 1cm (1/2in) border of flesh around the inside of each squash half. Mix the scooped-out squash with the filling and pop it all back into the grooves you have just carved out. Sprinkle over the lemon rind and roast in the oven for a further 10 minutes. Serve with a delicious crisp salad, such as Green Bean Salad with Roasted Fennel, Garlic & Mint (*see* page 74).

1 red onion, finely sliced
1 tbsp white wine vinegar
200g (7oz) sprouted lentils, or
   other mixed bean sprouts or
   mixed pea and bean sprouts
   (*see* My Secret, below)
200g (7oz) spinach leaves
1 red chilli, seeds removed
   and finely sliced
8 cherry tomatoes, cut in half
2 tbsp roughly chopped
   fresh coriander

1 tbsp roughly chopped
   mint leaves
seeds of 1 pomegranate
2 tbsp olive oil
1 tsp English mustard
1 tsp cumin seeds, toasted
   (*see* page 171)
1 tsp clear honey
juice of 1 lemon or lime
good pinch of salt and pepper

Lentil salad with toasted cumin dressing

This salad is packed with goodness, with its sprouted lentils mixed with red onions, spinach and pomegranate seeds, and all tossed with a toasted cumin dressing. I'm using green lentils (green mung beans), which are easy to sprout yourself, but it does take some time. If you would rather save yourself the hassle, then just buy a pack of mixed bean sprouts, or mixed pea and bean sprouts, instead.

Mix the red onion and white wine vinegar together in a non-metallic glass or ceramic bowl. Set aside while you prepare the other ingredients. The onions will start to release their colour and turn beautifully pink.

Toss the sprouts with the spinach, chilli, tomatoes, fresh coriander, mint and pomegranate seeds in a large bowl. Add the onions and mix well.

Make the dressing by whisking the remaining ingredients together. Pour over the salad, toss to combine and serve piled high for a great meal packed with superfoods.

· MY SECRET ·
Sprouting lentils is easy but it takes time. Rinse them thoroughly and leave to soak overnight. Drain, rinse and leave to sprout in a colander, covered with a clean, dark tea towel. Rinse and drain them every morning and night, moving them around to sprout evenly, until they are as sprouted as you like them.

SERVES 4
Prep time 20 minutes
Cook time 15 minutes

olive oil, for greasing and drizzling
250g (9oz) ricotta cheese
1 red chilli, seeds removed if you
    don't want it fiery (optional)
grated rind and juice of 1/2 lemon
1 spring onion, finely sliced
2 garlic cloves, finely chopped
1 tbsp roughly chopped chives,
    plus extra to garnish
good pinch of sea salt and pepper

1 small naan bread, about 50g
    (1³/₄oz)
1 tbsp freshly grated Parmesan
    cheese
1 tbsp mixed unsalted nuts
    (optional)
4 peppers, preferably Romano, cut
    in half lengthways and deseeded
aged balsamic vinegar, for drizzling
    (optional)

Stuffed sweet peppers

I think we've all had our fair share of bad stuffed peppers. Usually, they are loaded with rice and veg and baked until soft and often lifeless. This version doesn't have a grain of rice in sight and instead uses creamy ricotta to add a little indulgence. I've also topped them with some breadcrumbs made from leftover naan bread, but just use whatever bread you have – a little stale is good! The best peppers for this are the long, sweet Romano ones, but the regular ones will do.

Preheat the oven to 220°C/425°F/Gas Mark 7 and grease a baking sheet with a little oil.

Make the stuffing for the peppers by mixing together the ricotta, chilli (if using), lemon juice, spring onion, garlic, chives and salt and pepper in a bowl.

Make the topping by blitzing the naan bread, Parmesan, mixed nuts (if using) and lemon rind together in a food processor until finely ground.

Fill the peppers generously with the ricotta mixture and sprinkle over the breadcrumb mix. Set on the baking sheet and bake in the oven for 15 minutes. You may need to loosely cover them with foil if the breadcrumbs start to colour too much.

Remove from the oven, garnish with the chives and drizzle with olive oil and balsamic vinegar if you like. This is a stuffed pepper you will be proud of.

SERVES 4
Prep time 10 minutes
Cook time 1¹/₄ hours

3 red chillies, 2 for roasting whole
  and 1, thinly sliced, to garnish
3 tbsp oil – I like rapeseed oil or
  light olive oil
2 onions, finely sliced
2 bay leaves
1 tsp cumin seeds
1 tbsp garam masala
3 carrots, chopped into small
  bite-sized pieces
2 celery sticks, chopped into
  small bite-sized pieces
2 garlic cloves, finely chopped

300g (10¹/₂oz) dried lentils – I like
  green or brown lentils – washed,
  soaked in water for 30 minutes,
  then drained
1.5 litres (2³/₄ pints) hot vegetable
  stock
100g (3¹/₂oz) broccoli florets or
  baby broccoli
2 handfuls of spinach leaves
juice of ¹/₂ lemon, or to taste
sea salt and pepper
4 tbsp thick low-fat Greek yogurt,
  to garnish

Spiced vegetable soup with lentils & roasted chilli

Soups are the ultimate comfort food. I've made this dish hundreds of times and it never fails to hit the spot. You can use any vegetables you like, but I'm going for carrots, broccoli and spinach, and I'm using lentils to add some body to it. As I love chillies I'm adding them in two different ways – roasted and then fresh, but you don't need to roast them if you don't want to.

Start by roasting the chillies. If you have a gas hob, place a wire rack over the flames and roast your chillies on top until they are blistered and black. If not, use a preheated grill, making sure it is really hot. Keep turning the chillies so that they colour evenly. This should take about 5 minutes. Transfer to a bowl, cover with clingfilm and let cool.

While the chillies are roasting and cooling, start the soup. Gently heat 2 tablespoons of the oil in a large saucepan and fry the onions for about 10 minutes until they have turned light golden brown. Take half out and set aside. Cook the onions in the pan for a further 5 minutes, or until they are deep golden brown and crispy. These are for sprinkling over at the end. Take these out of the pan and reserve.

Pour the remaining tablespoon of oil into the pan and add the bay leaves and cumin seeds. Put the softened onions back in (that's the first set you took out of the pan) and add the garam masala, carrots, celery, garlic and lentils. Carefully peel the charred skin off the chillies, roughly chop (with or without seeds, it's up to you) and add to the soup. Stir well and leave to cook for 5 minutes before pouring in the hot stock. Bring the soup to a simmer and allow to cook for 40 minutes, or until the carrots and lentils have softened.

Remove from the heat and blitz a few times using a stick blender. I like to leave some texture in there. Put back on the heat and stir in the broccoli. After 2 minutes, stir in the spinach and turn off the heat. Taste the soup and adjust the seasoning and lemon juice.

Serve topped with a cooling dollop of yogurt, the reserved crispy onions and the sliced chilli.

SERVES 4
Prep time 15 minutes,
plus (preferably) chilling
Cook time around 8 minutes

2 tbsp vegetable oil
2 tsp cumin seeds
3 spring onions, finely sliced
2 garlic cloves, finely chopped
1 red chilli, finely chopped
1 tsp smoked paprika
400g (14oz) can mixed beans,
    drained and roughly mashed

2 tbsp roughly chopped
    fresh coriander
2 tbsp roughly chopped chives
good pinch of salt and pepper
4 burger buns, to serve

Spicy bean burgers

Most meat lovers would never pick a bean burger, but this is a great recipe packed with flavour for those meat-free days. Make sure you use ready-cooked canned mixed beans, as it saves so much time and effort in soaking dried beans and then boiling them up. And remember that beans are quite bland, so I've been bold with my flavours and spices.

Gently heat half the oil in a small frying pan and add the cumin seeds. When they start to sizzle, stir in the spring onions, garlic and chilli, and allow to fry for 30 seconds before sprinkling in the smoked paprika. Add a splash of water to stop it from burning. When all the water has evaporated, pour the mixture into the mashed beans in a bowl. Add the fresh coriander, chives and salt and pepper, and mix well.

Form the bean mixture into burger shapes. Lay on a plate, cover and pop in the fridge for 30 minutes to firm up, if you have time.

When you are ready to cook, gently heat the remaining oil in a frying pan and fry the chilled burgers for a few minutes on each side, only turning them over when they are golden brown. Serve in a burger bun, along with all your favourite trimmings.

I like to make large batches of these burgers and freeze some for another day. Just lay the uncooked burgers on a baking sheet and pop in the freezer instead of the fridge. Once the burgers are firm, you can then pack them together in a freezer-proof container or bag and freeze until you need them. To cook from frozen, preheat the oven to 180°C/350°F/Gas Mark 4, place the burgers on a baking sheet and cook for 30–35 minutes, or until cooked through.

Prep time 10 minutes,
plus cooling
Cook time 30 minutes

400g (14oz) potatoes, cut into
    small pieces
1/2 tsp ground turmeric
rind, pared in large pieces,
    and juice of 1 lemon
3 tbsp vegetable oil
1 tsp black mustard seeds
3 fat garlic cloves, finely chopped

1 tsp peeled and finely chopped
    fresh root ginger
really good pinch of chilli powder
2 tbsp finely chopped fresh coriander
100g (3 1/2oz) fresh or frozen peas,
    run under boiling water
3 tbsp semolina
salt

Aloo tikkis

*This is a recipe for traditional
Indian potato cakes – mashed
potatoes delicately spiced
and filled with peas and then
pan-fried until golden and
crispy. They are often served
with chutneys, so rummage
through the pantry and get
some of your favourites out.
I prefer to stuff the mash with
peas, but you can stir them
through if you like. It's worth
rolling them in semolina to get
them really crispy, but they
still taste great without.*

· MY SECRET ·
I like to pop my
tikkis in the fridge for
about 30 minutes after
I've formed them, to give
them time to firm up so
that they hold their shape
better after frying.

Fill a saucepan with cold water, add the potatoes with the turmeric,
a few large pieces of lemon rind and a good pinch of salt and bring
to the boil. Cook for about 15 minutes, or until the potatoes are soft.

Drain the potatoes and leave to steam and dry out in the colander
while you temper the spices and the holy trinity of garlic, ginger and
chilli. Gently heat 1 tablespoon of the oil in a frying pan and add the
mustard seeds. When they start to jump out of the pan, stir through
the garlic, ginger and chilli powder.

Transfer the potatoes to a bowl and pour the tempered spices over
the top. Add a good pinch of salt, squeeze over the lemon juice and
stir in the fresh coriander. Taste and add more chilli powder if you
like it fiery.

Using a fork, mash the potatoes and spread them out so that they
cool quickly. When they are cool enough to handle, start making
the tikkis by putting around a tablespoonful of mash in your hand
and flattening it out. Get around a teaspoonful of the blanched
peas and put them in the centre. Wrap the mashed potatoes around
them as if the peas were a stuffing. Flatten it slightly, making sure
the peas don't push their way through. Continue to make tikkis
until you have used up all the mash and peas.

Gently heat the remaining oil in a large frying pan. Roll the tikkis
in the semolina and pan-fry, in batches, on all sides until golden
and crispy. Keep the cooked ones warm in the oven while you
fry the rest. Serve with your favourite chutney such as Tomato
Chutney (*see* page 32).

SERVES 4 AS A SIDE
Prep time 5 minutes
Cook time 45 minutes

600g (1lb 5oz) potatoes (any sort will do), skins left on and scrubbed
1 tsp ground turmeric
1 dried chipotle chilli or 1 tsp chipotle chilli paste
1 tbsp white urad dhal (optional)
2 tsp fenugreek seeds
2 tbsp vegetable oil or light olive oil
2 tsp black mustard seeds
2 tsp cumin seeds
1 tsp smoked paprika

3 garlic cloves, finely sliced
3 spring onions, finely sliced
pinch of sea salt, or to taste
juice of 1 lime, plus extra lime halves for squeezing over

To garnish
2 tbsp chopped fresh coriander
2 heaped tbsp salted peanuts, roughly chopped

Spicy smoky potatoes

I first tasted potatoes like this at one of my favourite restaurants when I moved to London. They were divine – charred in all the right places with a hint of smokiness and suitably spicy. They had a strange crunch to them that I soon figured out was fried lentils (in this case white urad dhal), so I have added these and a little more crunch right at the end in the form of peanuts, but if you don't fancy them, just leave them out.

· MY SECRET ·
A chipotle chilli is a smoked jalapeño and is quite fiery. If you don't have any, just use a little extra smoked paprika, along with a fresh chilli if you want some heat.

Fill a saucepan with cold water, add the potatoes with the turmeric and chipotle chilli and bring to the boil, then cook until soft. Depending on how large the potatoes are, this could take up to 30 minutes. Drain them once they are soft, reserving the boiled softened chipotle chilli if you used one.

Gently heat a heavy-based frying pan and toast the urad dhal (if using) and fenugreek seeds until nutty and fragrant and starting to turn golden brown. Pour over the oil and add the mustard and cumin seeds. Once they start to sizzle, add the smoked paprika, garlic and spring onions, and allow them to soften for a minute or so. Finely chop the reserved chipotle chilli (if you used one) and stir this through. Add the potatoes and use a fork to break them up slightly.

Season with a little salt, remembering you are going to sprinkle over some salted peanuts later, and squeeze over the lime juice. Taste and adjust the seasoning. To make this dish extra crunchy, leave the potatoes to cook and slightly catch on the base of the pan. Stir them every now and again until crispy and golden brown all over.

Serve sprinkled with the fresh coriander and salted nuts, with lime halves to squeeze over, for an ultimate veggie side dish.

SERVES 4
Prep time 15 minutes
Cook time 5 minutes per
batch of fritters

Fritters
100g (3½oz) gram (chickpea) flour
1 tsp baking powder
1 tsp smoked paprika
1 tsp cumin seeds
good pinch of salt and pepper
2 eggs, beaten
75ml (2½fl oz) milk
200g (7oz) sweetcorn, drained if
  canned or defrosted if frozen
2 spring onions, finely sliced
2 garlic cloves, finely chopped
1–2 red chillies, finely sliced
1 tbsp roughly chopped chives
2 tbsp vegetable oil, plus extra
  as needed

Avocado salsa
1 avocado, peeled, stone removed
  and roughly chopped
1 red onion, finely chopped
6 cherry tomatoes or 1 large
  tomato, finely chopped
1 tbsp roughly chopped mint
good pinch of sea salt, or to taste
good drizzle of clear honey
juice of 1 lime, or to taste

Sweetcorn fritters with avocado salsa

I'm not a big fan of the word fritter, but I can't think of another name for these. They are like veggie-packed savoury pancakes, and if you have time to make the salsa I highly recommend it. I have used gram (chickpea) flour, which is gluten free, but you can use plain flour if you don't have any.

This recipe is like a ray of sunshine – so refreshing and light. It's great to have for brunch or a healthy snack.

Make the batter for the fritters by mixing together the flour, baking powder, smoked paprika, cumin seeds and salt and pepper in a bowl. In another bowl, whisk together the eggs and milk before pouring it into the dry mix. Beat together well until smooth and leave to stand while you prepare the rest of the ingredients.

Mix the sweetcorn, spring onions, garlic, chilli and chives together in a separate bowl. Add enough of the batter to coat them well – they should be a dropping consistency.

Heat a frying pan with the oil, then add around 2 tablespoonfuls of the batter mixture per fritter to the hot oil and cook for about 3 minutes until light golden brown on the underside before flipping over and cooking the other side for a couple of minutes. Keep the cooked fritters warm in the oven while you fry the rest, adding more oil to coat the base of the pan if you need to.

In the meantime, make the salsa by mixing all the ingredients together in a serving bowl, tasting and adjusting the flavourings as necessary. Serve with the warm fritters.

Kitchen gadgets

I love kitchen gadgets and seem to have them stuffed into every nook and cranny in my kitchen. When I moved house I realized just how many I had collected and shockingly discovered that many of them were unused and still had their tags attached! There are a few that I turn to time and time again to make my life simpler, and I know if I didn't have them I would have to work a lot harder in the kitchen.

SPICE BOX

I don't know what I would do without my spice box: the perfect, compact place to store those little gems of flavour. Not only will storing spices in a box or tin help them stay fresher for longer, but keeping them together allows you to free up much needed space in that overflowing storecupboard. To find out what I keep in my spice box, *see* pages 36–41.

SPICE GRINDER

Some spices can't be ground easily in a pestle and mortar, such as cinnamon bark and nutmeg. If you want to get into making your own garam masalas (*see* page 171) then you need to grind spices to a fine powder, which requires a lot of elbow grease. I bought my spice grinder quite cheaply and it hasn't failed me yet.

PESTLE & MORTAR

Every kitchen needs a pestle and mortar, if only for somewhere to drop your keys when you walk into the kitchen! I use my pestle and mortar for bashing, grinding, mixing, blending and a whole lot more. It's my favourite piece of kitchen kit and I couldn't live without it.

There are so many fancy pestle and mortars out there, but I like my good old heavy granite one. You can use a food processor instead but I prefer to grind my spices by hand so I can check how coarse they are.

MICROPLANE/GRATER

It is so much easier to grate garlic, ginger and citrus rind on a microplane than on a standard grater.

MINI CHOPPER/MINI FOOD PROCESSOR

Some ingredients need to be chopped very finely, which is great if you have good knife skills. If you want to cut your time in half it's best to pop them in a mini chopper and let the machine do all the work for you. It's great for puréeing tomatoes, onions, garlic, ginger and for making quick pastes and marinades.

STICK BLENDER

A nice-to-have, not a must-have, kitchen gadget that has more uses than you may think. I usually use mine to blitz veggies and lentils after cooking. I like the way using a stick blender allows you to control the texture of the final dish. For example, you can make your soups and dahl as smooth or as chunky as you like. I suggest using a stick blender for my Spiced Vegetable Soup with Lentils & Roasted Chilli and Black Dhal (*see* pages 100 and 140.)

SMALL ROLLING PIN

You can easily use a large rolling pin for making Indian breads such as rotis and parathas (*see* pages 144 and 149) but I prefer to use a traditional thin Indian one. My first kitchen gift was a small rolling pin and board for helping my grandmother make fresh rotis for dinner. My habits haven't changed and I love the control you have with a small pin – and it's also easier to store.

ELECTRIC WHISK

This is another nice-to-have gadget, and certainly not essential in an Indian kitchen. I love to bake and use my electric whisk a lot, but you can easily use a balloon whisk and a little muscle if you have time and are feeling strong.

CHAPTER 5

BBQ INDIAN SUMMER

SERVES 4
Prep time 10 minutes,
plus (preferably) chilling
Cook time 10 minutes

1 tbsp vegetable oil
1 tsp cumin seeds
3 spring onions, finely sliced
3 garlic cloves, finely chopped
2 dried red chillies, soaked in boiling
    water for 5 minutes, then drained
    and finely chopped
2 tsp garam masala
500g (1lb 2oz) minced beef
grated rind of 1 orange
1 egg, beaten
2 tbsp soft breadcrumbs – stale white
    bread is preferable but any will do,
    including naan (optional)
good pinch of salt and pepper
4 burger buns, to serve

Beetroot & carrot slaw
1 raw beetroot, grated
1 carrot, grated
1 tsp horseradish sauce
2 tbsp natural yogurt
juice of $1/2$ lemon, or to taste
good pinch of salt and pepper,
    or to taste

Blazing burgers

*You can't have a barbecue
without a burger, and I don't
mean regular boring burgers
that are crying out for some life.
I mean delicious, juicy, flavour-
filled ones. And you have to
have some slaw to go with it...*

Gently heat the oil in a frying pan and add the cumin seeds. When
they are sizzling, stir in the spring onions, garlic and chillies and
fry for 30 seconds before stirring in the garam masala. Turn off
the heat and allow the garam masala to cook in the residual heat.

In the meantime, mix together the beef, orange rind, egg,
breadcrumbs (if using) and salt and pepper in a bowl. Add the
fried spices and mix well. Form into burger shapes and pop in
the fridge for 30 minutes to firm up, if you have time.

Make the slaw by mixing all the ingredients together in a serving
bowl. Taste and adjust the seasoning.

Cook the burgers over a hot barbecue or in a hot griddle pan
or under a preheated high grill for a few minutes on each side,
flipping them often, or until cooked through to your liking.
Serve them inside a burger bun topped with slaw, along with
your favourite burger extras.

· MY SECRET ·
Sometimes I stuff my
burgers with a little
cheese, such as mozzarella
or blue cheese. It melts
perfectly in the middle of
the burger and oozes out
as you bite in.

SERVES 4
Prep time 5 minutes
Cook time 45 minutes

600g (1lb 5oz) new potatoes,
    halved if really large
1 tsp cumin seeds
1 tsp coriander seeds
1 dried red chilli
2 tbsp Mango Chutney (*see* page 167)
2 tbsp vegetable oil
a few rosemary sprigs
good pinch of sea salt, or to taste,
    plus extra (optional) for sprinkling

Glazed baby potatoes

I devised this dish when I had to visit Norway for work. I needed to come up with something that I could prepare in advance and that would be very different to what the people of the country would normally experience. It tastes sensational, so definitely give this a go if you fancy mixing up your roast potatoes recipe.

If cooking indoors, preheat the oven to 200°C/400°F/Gas Mark 6.

Fill a saucepan with cold water, add the potatoes and bring to the boil, then cook for about 15 minutes, or until cooked through.

Drain the potatoes in a colander and shake them well. Try and chuff up the edges as these will go crispy when roasted.

In the meantime, make the glaze. Coarsely crush the cumin, coriander seeds and chilli with a pestle and mortar. Mix the rest of the ingredients together and add the spices. Taste and adjust the seasoning.

Rub the glaze over the potatoes, wrap in foil and bake over a medium barbecue or in the oven for about 30 minutes. Serve sprinkled with a little extra salt if you like.

SERVES 4
Prep time 10 minutes
Cook time 35–45 minutes

8 –12 chicken drumsticks
lemon wedges, for squeezing over

Sticky chicken marinade
3 tbsp barbecue sauce –
   I like the hickory ones
2 tbsp soy sauce
2 tbsp clear honey
3 spring onions, finely chopped
3 garlic cloves, finely chopped
1 tbsp peeled and finely chopped
   fresh root ginger
1–2 red chillies, finely chopped
2 tbsp finely chopped fresh coriander

Harissa, mint & cumin marinade
2 tbsp thick natural yogurt
3 tbsp harissa

3 tbsp finely chopped mint
2 tbsp olive oil
2 tsp cumin seeds, roughly crushed
   with a pestle and mortar
2 tsp clear honey
juice of 1 lemon

Rosemary, coriander & garlic marinade
4 garlic cloves, finely chopped
a few rosemary sprigs,
   roughly chopped
3 tbsp roughly chopped
   fresh coriander
3 tsp coriander seeds, roughly
   crushed with a pestle and mortar
3 tbsp olive oil
good pinch of salt and pepper

Chicken drummers

I couldn't pick just one recipe, so I have shared three of my favourite marinades. If you have time, then these taste best when they have had time to marinate, so cover them and chill in the fridge for at least a few hours. But don't worry if you haven't the time – they will still taste delicious.

Make a few deep slashes in the drumsticks so that the flavours go right to the core.

Mix your chosen marinade ingredients together and rub all over the chicken in a glass or ceramic dish. Cover and leave to marinate in the fridge if you have time.

When ready to cook the drumsticks, cook over a hot barbecue for about 35 minutes, or place in a roasting tray and cook in an oven preheated to 200°C/400°F/Gas Mark 6 for 40–45 minutes, or until cooked through. Serve with lemon wedges.

FOLLOWING PAGE:
*Top left: Sticky chicken marinade
Bottom left: Rosemary,
coriander & garlic marinade
Bottom right: Harissa,
mint & cumin marinade*

SERVES 4
Prep time 15 minutes
Cook time 5 minutes

2 eggs
1 tsp chilli powder
1 tsp garlic paste
1/2 tsp ground turmeric
1/2 tsp black peppercorns,
   crushed with a pestle
   and mortar
good pinch of salt

3 tbsp plain flour
75g (2³/₄oz) desiccated coconut
75g (2³/₄oz) panko breadcrumbs
20 raw king prawns, shells removed
   but tails left on, deveined
2 tbsp vegetable oil
juice of 1 lime, plus extra lime
   wedges for squeezing over

Coconut-crusted prawns

I have always been fond of seafood and it seems to taste so much better on the grill. This recipe requires a frying pan if you haven't got skewers, and it really doesn't make too much difference which method you use. If using wooden skewers, soak them in water for 30 minutes before using or they will burst into flames over the barbecue. I am using a mix of panko (Japanese-style) breadcrumbs as well as desiccated coconut to bread the prawns, but you can easily use regular breadcrumbs instead.

Beat the eggs with the chilli powder, garlic paste, turmeric, crushed peppercorns and salt in a bowl. Put the flour in a separate bowl. Mix the coconut and breadcrumbs together in another bowl.

Pané the prawns by tossing them in the flour, making sure they are evenly coated, then dip them in the egg mixture and then roll them in the breadcrumbs. It's best if you double pané them, so dip them again in the egg and then again in breadcrumbs.

If cooking in a frying pan, gently heat the pan on a cool part of the barbecue. Add the oil and then fry the prawns for a few minutes on each side. Once they are crispy and golden brown, drain on kitchen paper. If cooking on skewers, carefully skewer the prawns, trying not to lose too many breadcrumbs. Drizzle over the oil and cook over the flames, turning often, until crispy and golden brown.

Squeeze over the lime juice just before serving, with some extra wedges for lime lovers.

SERVES 4
Prep time 5 minutes,
plus marinating
Cook time up to 15 minutes

12 lamb chops, French trimmed
   if possible or trimmed of any fat
lime wedges, for squeezing over

Marinade
3 tbsp vegetable oil or light
   olive oil
1 tsp cumin seeds
1 tsp ground coriander

1 tsp ground turmeric
1/2 tsp chilli powder, or to taste
1 red chilli, finely chopped
   (optional)
2 fat garlic cloves, finely chopped
a few rosemary sprigs,
   roughly chopped
good pinch of sea salt
   and pepper, or to taste

Finger-licking chops

Lamb chops marinated in spices and rosemary – it says it all. One of my fondest memories is of munching on lamb chops when I visited family during my year travelling around the world after studying. I had spent all that time with people I'd never met, and happiness overcame me when my parents told me there were members of our family living in a remote part of Australia. It was barbecue season and they decided to present me with dish after dish of delicious food I had truly missed. I have been generous with the chilli, but you can reduce it if you aren't that keen.

Mix all the marinade ingredients together – you can add a little water if you need the marinade to go further. Taste and adjust the seasoning and heat if you think it needs it.

Rub the marinade all over the lamb chops in a dish, then cover and pop in the fridge to marinate for a few hours, if you have time.

When you are ready, cook the chops on a hot barbecue or under a preheated high grill, in batches, for up to 4 minutes on each side, or until cooked to your liking. I like my lamb pink, so I cook it for only 2 minutes on each side. Serve with lime wedges and some sides for a wonderful Indian summer feast.

SERVES 4
Prep time 5 minutes
Cook time 10–12 minutes
for fillets; 25–30 minutes
for a side of salmon

4 salmon fillets, about 150g (5¹/₂oz)
   each, or 1 large side of salmon,
   about 600g (1lb 5oz)

Spice paste
4 tbsp coconut cream (or grated
   fresh coconut if you find some)
2 tbsp natural yogurt
2 tbsp finely chopped fresh coriander
1 tbsp tamarind paste/concentrate,
   or to taste
small handful of fresh curry leaves
   (*see* My Secret, page 20) (optional)

1 tsp black mustard seeds
¹/₂ tsp ground turmeric
1 red chilli, deseeded if you
   wish, sliced
1 tbsp peeled and julienned
   fresh root ginger
good pinch of salt, or to taste –
   this dish has coastal flavours,
   so I prefer sea salt, but you
   can use regular table salt

Scented steamed fish

*This recipe was inspired by a
trip I made to the idyllic Indian
spice state of Kerala when I
became really serious about
cooking. I travelled around
with my mum learning about
spices – the first of many spice
trips we went on together. Some
of the best seafood dishes hail
from this region and they are
packed full of native spices
and herbs. A traditional way
to cook coastal dishes is in
banana leaves, which grow
in abundance in Kerala and
that I've been told are available
in some Asian stores. If you
haven't got any to hand (and I
rarely have), then just use some
nonstick baking paper soaked in
a little water. This will keep the
fish moist and won't catch fire
on the barbecue.*

Mix all the spice paste ingredients together in a bowl. Taste
and add a little more salt or tamarind if you think it needs it.

Rub the paste all over the fish, then wrap the fish in nonstick
baking paper or foil.

Cook over a medium barbecue or in an oven preheated to
180°C/350°F/Gas Mark 4 for 10–12 minutes, depending on the
thickness of the fillet, or for about 25–30 minutes if cooking a
whole side of salmon. The salmon tastes best when it is slightly
pink in the middle, so it's advisable to undercook it if you aren't
sure. You can always pop it back on or under the heat if you
need to. Serve with some delicious sides and salads.

· MY SECRET ·
The tamarind adds a sweet
and sour flavour to the fish,
but if you can't lay your hands
on any, add some freshly
squeezed lime juice and
sugar instead.

SERVES 4
Prep time 15 minutes,
plus (preferably) chilling
Cook time 10 minutes

400g (14oz) minced lamb
4 sun-dried tomatoes in oil,
    drained and finely chopped
1 tsp garam masala
1 tsp ground turmeric
1/2 tbsp fennel seeds
1 tsp cumin seeds
3 garlic cloves, finely chopped
1 tbsp peeled and finely chopped
    fresh root ginger

1–2 red chillies, finely chopped
grated rind and juice of 1 lemon
2 tbsp finely chopped fresh coriander
3 tbsp finely chopped mint leaves
2 tsp clear honey
good pinch of sea salt
long woody rosemary sprigs, for
    skewering, bottom leaves removed
lemon wedges, for squeezing over

Herby lamb kebabs

*You can find lamb kebabs
everywhere. The best I've ever
had was at a family wedding
in Baroda in Gujarat. They
were succulent, perfectly spiced
and loaded with herbs. This
is a recipe I created not long
after I returned and I've been
making them ever since. The
sun-dried tomatoes add a
summer vibe. If you can't
find woody rosemary to use
as skewers, you can use metal
or even wooden ones. Just
make sure you soak the
wooden ones for around
30 minutes in water before
using or they may catch fire!*

Mix all the ingredients except the lemon juice, rosemary sprigs
and lemon wedges together in a bowl.

Press the meat mixture on to the woody ends of the rosemary sprigs
and pop in the fridge for 30 minutes to firm up, if you have time.

Cook the kebabs over a medium barbecue or in a medium griddle
pan or under a preheated medium grill for about 10 minutes,
squeezing over the lemon juice while cooking and turning often,
or until cooked through. Serve with lemon wedges, along with
some Cucumber Raita (*see* page 166) to cool down any chilli heat.

· MY SECRET ·
You can use minced
pork, turkey or beef
instead of lamb. Using
the grated rind and juice
of 1 orange instead of
lemon adds a different
citrus note.

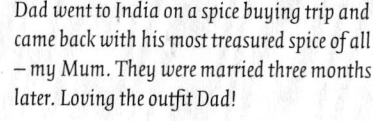

Dad went to India on a spice buying trip and came back with his most treasured spice of all — my Mum. They were married three months later. Loving the outfit Dad!

Mum on her wedding day, looking stunning.

Dad was always proud of the Patak's factory and never missed a moment to show off his and Mum's new recipe creations.

How '80's does this look?! When Mum joined the family business she soon became the face of Patak's and worked tirelessly developing new recipes, some of which are still sold today – you've gotta love our Tandoori Paste. I used to see this poster above reception at the office when I was young.

Dad on one of his business trips checking produce. He was meticulous and always kept a close eye on the quality of each and every ingredient that was used in the Patak's secret recipes.

Mum's grandparents (and dog) lived in Mumbai, but were both born in Ahmedabad, Gujarat. Mum learned a lot of her cooking skills from her grandmother.

SERVES 4
Prep time 2 minutes
Cook time 10 minutes

4 large corn on the cob, preferably
    in their husks
25g (1oz) butter, softened
1 tsp dried chilli flakes or 1 fresh red
    chilli, finely chopped, or to taste
good pinch of sea salt, or to taste,
    and pepper
grated rind and juice of 1 lime,
    or to taste

Scorched cobbed corn

This has to be one of the easiest recipes to make. It uses only a few ingredients yet tastes absolutely divine; you just can't beat corn being charred on a barbecue and brushed liberally with butter and chilli. You can find street vendors selling corn in their husks all over Asia and each area will have its own unique way of adding regional flair to it. I drew inspiration for this recipe from the beaches of Mumbai, where you can get some of the very best corn on the cob I've ever tried. If you can find corn cobs in their husks, then perfect, but prepared corn on the cob is absolutely fine to use.

Scorch the corn cobs on a hot barbecue, turning often, until they are charred.

In the meantime, make the basting butter by mixing the rest of the ingredients except the lime rind together. Give it a taste and add more chilli, salt or lime juice if you think it needs it.

Once the husks are nicely charred, carefully peel them back to reveal the cobs. Baste the corn cobs with the flavoured butter often and continue to cook until the kernels are tender and starting to colour evenly. Serve with extra flavoured butter and sprinkled with the lime rind.

· MY SECRET ·
If you have any leftovers, cut the corn off the cob and reheat in a smoking-hot pan for a few minutes. Toss in some fresh coriander and a squeeze of lime, and you have a quick corn salsa: great with nachos.

SERVES 4
Prep time 10 minutes
Cook time 1 hour 10 minutes

1.5kg (3lb 5oz) pork belly ribs,
  individual ribs or as a rack –
  try and get to the butcher for
  these for the best-quality meat
100ml (3½fl oz) apple juice

Dry rub
1 tbsp fennel seeds
1 tsp cumin seeds
1 tsp black peppercorns
1 tbsp smoked paprika

Marinade
200ml (7fl oz) passata
2 tbsp golden syrup
1 tbsp Worcestershire sauce
2 tsp English mustard
1 tsp oregano, finely chopped
  fresh or dried
1 tsp finely chopped garlic
50ml (2fl oz) apple juice
salt and pepper

Smokin' ribs

Ribs are always a favourite at barbecues, and the key is in the marinade. If you have a smoker, then def fire it up to really intensify the flavour. If you haven't, fear not because smoked paprika has a magical way of making everything taste like you did! This recipe has two parts: the dry rub, which is baked on to the ribs in the oven, and then the wet marinade, which is basted on when finishing them off on the barbecue. If the weather isn't playing ball, instead of basting the meat with the marinade, just pour it all over the ribs and pop it under the grill to char them.

Preheat the oven to 150°C/300°F/Gas Mark 2.

Using a pestle and mortar, bash the fennel and cumin seeds and peppercorns together for the dry rub. Stir in the smoked paprika and rub the spice mix all over the ribs. Place them in a roasting tray so that they fit in a single layer. Pour in the apple juice, cover tightly with foil and bake for 1 hour.

In the meantime, gently heat all the marinade ingredients in a saucepan. Taste and adjust the seasoning if you think it needs it. Reserve some of it to serve as a dipping sauce.

After an hour the ribs will be tender, so it's time to move to the barbecue. Smother the meat with some of the remaining marinade and place directly on the rack of a hot barbecue. Cook for 10 minutes, moving them around and basting with the marinade as often as you can. Serve the ribs with potato wedges, pickled veggies and the reserved marinade for dipping.

SERVES 4
Prep time 5 minutes
Cook time 2 minutes

Spice rubs, pastes & oil

Everyone needs some good spice rubs and pastes up their sleeve, and ideally ones that will go with a whole host of meats, seafood and veggies. I grew up learning all about garam masalas and which spices taste best with which ingredients. Our spice pastes have become legendary and I've picked up several secret tips along the way, especially when I used to do the spice grinding for the family products. Over the years I have bent a lot of these rules, so here are a few special spicing ideas of mine for you to try out when the barbecue season comes around. And as with all my recipes, if you haven't got an ingredient or two, then don't worry about it. Just use what you have and see how it turns out.

1 tsp coriander seeds
1 tsp cumin seeds
1 dried red chilli
$1/4$ tsp black peppercorns
$1/2$ tsp ground turmeric
good pinch of ground cinnamon
good pinch of ground cloves
(optional)
good pinch of sea salt
$1/2$ tsp your favourite dried
herbs (rosemary and mint
work well with lamb;
oregano with chicken)

Dry rub for meat

This basic rub works wonderfully with most meats. If you are going to have it with chicken, I suggest adding a little more coriander seed, and if using with lamb, then add a small quantity of fennel seeds. I like to roast my spices first but don't worry if you don't have time. It just releases more of the flavour. Gently massage the rub into your favourite meat and roast in the oven or on the barbecue.

Gently heat a heavy-based frying pan and toast the coriander and cumin seeds, chilli and peppercorns for a few minutes until fragrant and the seeds are golden brown.

Pour into a mortar and allow to cool for a few minutes, then grind well with a pestle. Toss in the remaining spices, salt and herbs and mix together. This dry spice rub will keep in an airtight container for a few weeks.

Wet paste for meat

To make the dry rub for meat into a paste, just add 1 teaspoon each crushed garlic and peeled and grated fresh root ginger with a little vegetable or rapeseed oil. This will keep happily in an airtight container in the fridge for at least 5 days.

Wet paste for seafood

1 tsp fennel seeds
$^1/_2$ tsp black mustard seeds
$^1/_4$ tsp cumin seeds
$^1/_4$ tsp ground turmeric
2 tbsp coconut cream or 1 tbsp
    desiccated coconut and
    1 tbsp natural yogurt
1 tsp garlic paste
1 tsp tamarind paste/
    concentrate (optional)
grated rind and juice of 1 lime
good pinch of sea salt,
    or to taste, and pepper
pinch of sugar (optional)

Making a paste for coating seafood is a great way to enhance their delicate flavours. I borrow southern Indian ingredients to create a simple paste that is perfect for all types of seafood. Rub on your favourite seafood and roast in the oven or on the barbecue.

Mix all the ingredients together and taste. Add more salt and even a pinch of sugar to balance it out if you think it needs it.

Put into an airtight container, pop in the fridge and use within 3 days.

Spiced oil for veggies

a few tbsp olive oil
$^1/_2$ tsp cumin seeds
$^1/_4$ tsp coriander seeds
good pinch of dried chilli flakes
$^1/_4$ tsp ground turmeric
good pinch of salt and pepper

I love vegetables just as they are, but adding this spiced oil to them can make them taste truly exciting. Simply rub on your chosen veggies and then roast in the oven or on the barbecue.

Mix all the ingredients together and put into an airtight container. This infused oil will keep for around a month.

Fridge favourites

There are a few essential fresh ingredients that I like to keep on hand to help me lift the flavour of my dishes. The fresher the better...

THE HOLY TRINITY — GARLIC, GINGER & FRESH CHILLIES

I don't think I need to explain why these three ingredients are so important. I don't know what I would do without fresh garlic, ginger and chillies in my life. As well as using them chopped, I also like to grate them and make my own garlic and ginger paste (purée) – easy peasy with a mini chopper/food processor (*see* page 111).

If I know I am going away and have any of these left in my fridge, I grate them into separate ice cube trays, topping each compartment with water and then a thin layer of oil before freezing. Then, whenever I need them, I simply pop out a cube. I also freeze my chillies in an airtight bag and chop them from frozen.

There are so many different types of chillies and all freeze well – see what I've written about my favourite ones on pages 88–9.

When buying fresh garlic look closely to see if it has roots growing out of the top. If it does it means it's old and won't taste fresh.

Ginger should be heavy and the skin shouldn't be wrinkly. Break a little off and check it feels moist, as it will last so much longer if it does.

FRESH CORIANDER

Although you can grow this easily I have never had much luck and so I buy fresh coriander bunches and keep them in my fridge. To keep it looking fresh and bright, wrap the stalks in some damp kitchen paper. Try with Avocado & Coriander Salsa (*see* page 25).

CURRY LEAVES

I grew up with a fresh curry leaf plant in my kitchen so we were never short of fresh curry leaves. You can buy them dried but I'm not a fan and prefer to leave them out if I don't have fresh leaves to hand. When you do find them, make sure you buy a few extra bunches and pop them in the freezer. They freeze amazingly well and you will always have them when you need them. Be sure to always thoroughly wash them under clean, cold running water before adding to recipes or freezing.

Crisped up in a little oil, fresh curry leaves make a wonderful garnish for topping many spiced dishes. Try with Charred Baby Aubergines or Salty Masala Lassi (*see* pages 20 and 205).

ONIONS
I go through onions like you wouldn't believe. I always keep spring onions and red onions in my fridge for raw dishes, and I use white or brown onions for cooking. I'm sure I don't need to tell you that if they are sprouting roots, you have held onto them too long.

Transform the humble onion into Carrot, Onion & Spinach Bhajias or a versatile Caramelized Onion & Balsamic Chutney (*see* pages 14 and 161).

YOGURT
My grandmother used to make her own yogurt, which always tasted better than what we could buy, but I never make my own and so natural yogurt is on my shopping list every week.

Yogurt is great as a low-fat thickener as well as a good substitute for cream in those indulgent desserts, including Pomegranate & Ricotta Frozen Yogurt (*see* page 190). You can mix it with other ingredients to transform it into a tasty dressing for salads, or drizzle unadulterated on spiced, savoury dishes, such as Papri Chaat (*see* page 30). Also a key ingredient in classic Cucumber Raita (*see* page 166).

LEMON/LIME
I like to balance the flavour of a lot of my recipes with some citrus and always have lemons and limes to hand. Their juice and zesty flavour brings out the spice flavours in a way I can't explain.

CHAPTER

6

THOSE LITTLE EXTRAS

SERVES 4–6
Prep time 10 minutes,
plus soaking
Cook time 2 hours

· MY SECRET ·
Mash boiled lentils
with the back of a spoon
or pulse a few times using a
stick blender. It will make
the dish a little creamier,
especially if you stir
through some yogurt
at the end.

200g (7oz) dried black urad dhal,
  washed in several changes of water
2 small onions or large shallots,
  finely sliced
1 tsp ground turmeric
4 black cardamom pods (optional)
1 cinnamon stick
2–3 green chillies, slit down the
  middle but left whole
3 tbsp vegetable oil (this recipe tastes
  best made with ghee/clarified
  butter – do as you wish)
2 tsp cumin seeds

2 fat garlic cloves, finely chopped
1 tbsp peeled and julienned fresh
  root ginger
2 tsp coriander seeds
1/2 tsp ground asafoetida/hing
  (optional)
2 tbsp tomato purée
10 cherry tomatoes, cut in half
good pinch of salt, or to taste

To garnish
lots of chopped fresh coriander
a few tbsp natural yogurt

Black dhal

*I'm all about the short cuts
and love creating meals that
are simple and quick. However,
this recipe is not one of those.
It's a labour of love, but it truly
is worth all the effort. The best
black dhal (lentils) I've ever had
(rumoured to be the best in the
world) was from the Bukhara
restaurant in Delhi. They say
they cook it for over 40 hours
– no wonder it tastes so good!
Oh, and they add a lot more fat
than I have here. I don't have
40 hours and so this will never
taste as good as theirs, but it
sure hits the spot when I'm
craving it.*

*You can find black urad dhal,
or black lentils, at all Asian
shops and I do recommend that
you hunt it out. Sadly there
really isn't a suitable substitute.*

Soak the lentils overnight (or for at least 8 hours) in plenty of cold water. The next day, drain off the water and wash again a few times until the water runs clear. Pour the lentils into a saucepan with plenty of cold water (around 1 litre/1 3/4 pints will do) and add half the onions or shallots, the turmeric, black cardamoms (if using), cinnamon stick and chillies. Bring to the boil, then reduce the heat and allow to simmer for 1 1/2 hours, or until the lentils are tender, topping up with more water if necessary.

Make the tadka – the scented oil that adds flavour to the dhal – by gently heating the oil in a frying pan and adding half the cumin seeds. When they are sizzling, stir in the garlic, ginger and remaining onions or shallots. Cook for 2 minutes while you finely crush the remaining cumin seeds and the coriander seeds with a pestle and mortar. Stir this into the frying pan with the asafoetida/hing (if using), tomato purée and tomatoes. Add a splash of water, stir well and allow the spices to cook for a few minutes.

Pour the tadka into the cooked dhal. Add a really good pinch of salt and bubble for 5 minutes to release the tadka flavours. Taste and adjust the seasoning if you need to. You can add more chilli if you like yours hot.

Serve garnished with lots of fresh coriander and a little yogurt.

SERVES 4
Prep time 5 minutes
Cook time 30 minutes

500g (1lb 2oz) carrots, cut into
    halves or quarters lengthways,
    depending on the thickness
    of your carrots
2 tbsp olive oil
1 tsp caraway seeds
good pinch of salt

good pinch of cracked
    black peppercorns
a few thyme sprigs –
    I love lemon thyme
1 tsp unsalted butter
good drizzle of clear honey

Caraway glazed carrots

This dish used to make
a regular appearance at
Sunday lunch when I was a
kid. My dad would take us
all for a bike ride and then we
would spend what was left
of the morning cooling off
at the local swimming pool.
We would return home just in
time to see my mum putting
the finishing touches to family
lunch before tucking into a
well-deserved meal. After a
snooze on the sofa it was time
for dessert. I miss Sundays
with my family... but at least
I can recreate the dishes to bring
back the memories. If you can't
lay your hands on caraway
seeds, use cumin or coriander
seeds to add a little earthiness
to the dish.

Preheat the oven to 200°C/400°F/Gas Mark 6.

Mix all the ingredients except the honey together, spread
out in a roasting tray and roast for about 25 minutes, or until
soft and crisping up at the edges.

Drizzle over the honey and roast for a further 5 minutes.
Perfect with any roast dinner or as a side dish to any meal.

MAKES 8
Prep time 10 minutes,
plus proving
Cook time around 15 minutes

250g (9oz) wholewheat flour
(chapatti atta), plus extra
for dusting
2 tbsp vegetable oil

good pinch of salt
around 100ml (3½ fl oz) warm water
butter or ghee (clarified butter),
for brushing (optional)

· MY SECRET ·
Sometimes I brush my rotis
with flavoured butter –
I love garlic and coriander
butter and also rosemary
and chilli butter.

Classic roti

*I grew up with fresh hot rotis
(also known as chapattis),
and I've been making them
ever since I was little. A roti
is a traditional unleavened
bread from northern India,
cooked in a dry pan. It can
then be brushed with butter
or ghee (clarified butter) if you
want to be indulgent. This
recipe uses wholewheat flour,
available from all Asian shops
and called chapatti atta, but
if you can't find it, just use
ordinary wholemeal flour,
or even plain flour if you wish.
This is a great basic dough,
which means it's perfect for
adding flavours and spices to.
My recipe is classically plain.*

Mix the flour, oil and salt together in a large bowl. Pour in enough
of the warm water to make a dough. The dough shouldn't be sticky
or dry. Knead for a few minutes on a lightly floured work surface
and then return the dough to the bowl, cover with clingfilm and
allow to rest for 30 minutes.

Heat a large, heavy-based frying pan over a fairly high heat and start
rolling out the rotis. Divide the dough into 8 equal pieces. Sprinkle
your work surface and rolling pin with a little more flour. Roll each
dough ball into a circle a few millimetres thick. Sprinkle the dough
with more flour if it begins to stick. Dust off any excess flour from a
roti and place it in the pan. When little bubbles form on the top, flip
the roti over to cook the other side. Use a spatula or rolled-up clean
tea towel to press the roti against the heat of the pan.

Once the roti is golden brown on both sides, transfer to a warm
plate and brush with butter or ghee, if you wish – there is no need
to pre-melt it, as it will melt when it touches the hot roti. Cover with
a clean tea towel while you make the rest. There's nothing like fresh
hot bread, so serve these straight away.

SERVES 4
Prep time 10 minutes
Cook time 35–40 minutes

2 tbsp light olive oil
2 tsp garam masala
1/4 tsp dried chilli flakes
2 heaped tbsp soft white
   breadcrumbs
2 garlic cloves, finely chopped

juice of 1/2 lemon
200g (7oz) cauliflower,
   broken into florets
300g (10 1/2 oz) broccoli,
   broken into florets
good pinch of salt and pepper

· MY SECRET ·
Any robust greens
work well here, so try
adding Brussels sprouts,
cut in half, to add some
extra nuttiness to your
side dish.

Crunchy roast cauliflower & broccoli

*I love this recipe. Roast
cauliflower and broccoli
with ingredients they
love and they will taste
just amazing.*

Preheat the oven to 200°C/400°F/Gas Mark 6.

Mix all the ingredients together and spread out on a baking sheet
in a single layer. Roast for 35–40 minutes until crunchy and starting
to colour around the edges. Make sure you scoop up all the crispy
roasted breadcrumbs before serving with your favourite Big Bite
(*see* pages 42–69).

SERVES 4
Prep time 5 minutes
Cook time 45 minutes

· MY SECRET ·
You can make extra
spice paste and keep
it in your fridge for about
a week. If you omit the
garlic, it will keep for
about a month.

900g (2lb) roasting potatoes
  (any will do), cut into large
  bite-sized pieces

Spice paste
1 tbsp cumin seeds
2 tsp coriander seeds

½ tsp black peppercorns
2 dried red chillies
2 fat garlic cloves, peeled
  good pinch of sea salt
4 tbsp oil – rapeseed oil
  or light olive oil is great

Cumin roast potatoes

*These are roasties with a
difference. If you have any
leftover spice pastes rolling
around in your cupboards,
then this is perfect for using
them up and adding some
extra flavour to an all-time
favourite. One of the best
bits of a roast dinner is the
potatoes, especially if they are
crispy on the outside and fluffy
on the inside. Every Sunday
my mother would make these
using one of our spice pastes,
but if you don't have any to
hand, then here is a paste you
can easily make up yourself.*

Preheat the oven to 200°C/400°F/Gas Mark 6.

Fill a large saucepan with cold water, add the potatoes and bring
to the boil, then cook for around 20 minutes, or until soft.

In the meantime, make the spice paste. Coarsely crush the cumin
and coriander seeds, peppercorns and chillies with a pestle and
mortar. Add the garlic cloves and sea salt and pound together,
then work in half the oil to make a paste.

Drain the potatoes in a colander and chuff them up so that the
edges will go really crispy in the oven. Put a large roasting tray
(large enough so that the potatoes will sit in a single layer) directly
on the hob, add the remaining oil and gently heat before tipping
in the potatoes. Stir well and leave for 1 minute, then turn off the
heat and add the spice paste. Toss the potatoes well to coat, then
transfer the tray to the oven to crisp up for around 20 minutes.

SERVES 4
Prep time 2 minutes,
plus soaking
Cook time 10 minutes

300g (10¹/₂oz) white basmati rice,
    washed in several changes of
    water and left to soak in cold
    water for around 30 minutes
    if you have time
1 cinnamon stick
1 blade of mace (optional)
2 bay leaves

4 cloves
4 green cardamom pods
1 tsp cumin seeds
2 black cardamom pods (optional)
good pinch of saffron threads
    (optional)
good pinch of salt
2 tbsp vegetable oil

Foolproof pilau rice

*Cooking rice always worries
people. There are two main
ways of getting perfect rice:
either letting the rice absorb
every drop of water, or draining
off any excess once it's cooked.
Personally, I prefer the latter,
as it works every time and you
never have to deal with burnt rice
stuck to the bottom of your pan.*

*I'm using basmati rice for its
flavour and the heavenly scent
that fills my kitchen during
cooking. If you have time, then
try and soak the grains for half
an hour. It allows them to
lengthen so that you maximize
their beautiful flavour, but don't
leave them any longer, as they
will soften too much and break
up when you boil them. You can
use this as a base recipe and add
lots of different spices or leave it
plain if you prefer.*

Fill a saucepan with plenty of cold water and bring it to the boil.
Drain the rice and add it to the water with all the spices and salt.
Stir well and pour in the oil. Stir again before leaving it to cook
for 7 minutes, or until al dente – it should have a little bite to it.

Drain off the water and allow the rice to steam for a minute in the
colander or sieve. If you aren't serving it right away, then a foolproof
way of keeping it fluffy and hot is to put some foil over the sieve.
Pour some water into the rice pan and put the sieve on top. Gently
heat the water and leave the rice to steam until you are ready for it.

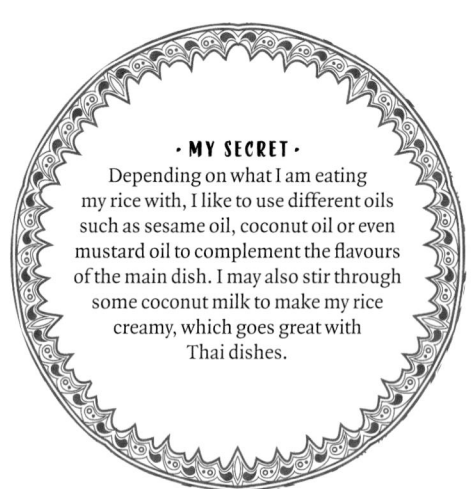

· MY SECRET ·
Depending on what I am eating
my rice with, I like to use different oils
such as sesame oil, coconut oil or even
mustard oil to complement the flavours
of the main dish. I may also stir through
some coconut milk to make my rice
creamy, which goes great with
Thai dishes.

MAKES 8
Prep time 20 minutes,
plus proving
Cook time 20 minutes

250g (9oz) wholewheat flour
(chapatti atta – *see* page 144),
plus extra for dusting
2 tbsp finely chopped mint leaves
1 tsp cumin seeds
1/2 tsp chilli powder, or more
if you love yours hot

2 fat garlic cloves, finely chopped
4 tbsp vegetable oil, plus extra
for cooking
good pinch of salt
around 100ml (31/2fl oz) warm water
butter or ghee (clarified butter),
for brushing (optional)

Flaky mint & chilli paratha

Parathas are flaky breads made from wholemeal flour or plain flour. The flaky layers are created by adding oil, butter or ghee (clarified butter) to the dough at different stages. They can be any shape you like, but I'm opting for round. You can leave them plain, add spices and herbs to the dough like I have or even stuff them with spiced veggies (see page 150). Personally, I prefer adding a few simple ingredients to give the bread some life, and then dipping it into a fresh hot chai (see page 213). My ideal weekend breakfast.

Mix together the flour, mint, cumin, chilli powder, garlic, most of the oil and the salt in a large bowl. Pour in enough of the warm water to make a dough. The dough shouldn't be sticky or dry. Knead for a few minutes on a lightly floured work surface and then return to the bowl, cover with clingfilm and allow to rest for 30 minutes.

Divide the dough into 8 equal pieces. Sprinkle your work surface and rolling pin with a little more flour and roll each dough ball into a circle a few millimetres thick. Sprinkle the dough with more flour if it begins to stick. Brush a little of the remaining oil on top of the dough and roll up into a cigar shape. Grab one end, lift the dough up and slap it on to the work surface to lengthen it. Grab the other end and do the same until it is around 50cm (20in) long. Rub a little more oil over the dough and roll it up so that it looks like a coil, tucking the ends into the middle to hold its shape. Brush the top with a little more oil and allow to rest while you do the same with the other dough balls.

Sprinkle your work surface with a little flour and roll each coil to flatten them out into circles a little thicker than last time. If you have time, you can now repeat the rolling, lengthening, oiling, coiling and flattening process – each time you do this you add more layers, which will result in extra flaky parathas.

Heat a large, heavy-based frying pan over a medium heat. Dust off any excess flour from a flattened coil and place it in the pan. When little bubbles form on the top, flip the paratha over to cook the other side. Drizzle a little oil into the pan and use a spatula or rolled-up clean tea towel to press the paratha against the heat of the pan. Brush the top with a little more oil and flip back over for 30 seconds.

Once the paratha is golden brown on both sides, transfer to a warm plate and brush with butter or ghee, if you wish. Cover with a clean tea towel while you make the rest. If you've added enough oil to your parathas, you should be able to see the layers. You can always scrunch each one up a little to release them.

Stuffed parathas

Making a stuffed paratha is slightly different and it isn't flaky like the plain ones above. Make the stuffing first so that it has time to cool. I love simple stuffings like cabbage and peas, but you can use any cooked veggies. Add some flavour to them when sautéeing, such as ground turmeric, cumin seeds, ground coriander and the usual holy trinity of finely chopped garlic, ginger and chillies. Season to taste and you've got yourself a great stuffing. Make the dough as above and roll out into small discs before placing a good heaped tablespoon of cooled stuffing in the middle. Roll the edges up and press together so that the filling is enclosed within, making sure there are no gaps or your filling will fall out. Carefully roll out into a large circle, trying not to break the dough. Cook the parathas like the plain ones above, adding oil to make them crispy. They're a meal in themselves!

SERVES 4
Prep time 10 minutes
Cook time 45 minutes

2 large sweet potatoes, skins
    left on, scrubbed and cut
    in half lengthways
1 tbsp vegetable oil
1/2 tsp coriander seeds
good pinch of ground cinnamon
a few thyme sprigs

1 tbsp crème fraîche or
    natural yogurt
2 tbsp soft white breadcrumbs –
    I like naan breadcrumbs
2 tbsp freshly grated
    Parmesan cheese
sea salt and pepper

Sweet potato mash with a Parmesan crumb

Mash is one of my all-time favourite sides and I love any kind, especially sweet potato mash. This is a recipe that is a little more labour intensive than just boiling the potatoes and mashing them, but it is worth the bit of extra effort, which you will be thankful for with every bite. Friends are always impressed when I pop this on the table and they never believe me when I share the recipe, as it's so simple to make.

Preheat the oven to 200°C/400°F/Gas Mark 6.

Rub the sweet potatoes all over with the oil, coriander seeds, ground cinnamon, thyme and a good pinch of salt and pepper. Put on a baking sheet, cut-side up, and roast in the oven for 40 minutes, or until soft.

Take the potatoes out of the oven and turn the oven to grill if it has that function, or preheat a grill to medium. Scoop out all the flesh, trying not to tear the crispy skins, and stir through the crème fraîche or yogurt. Taste and adjust the seasoning before putting the potato back in the skins. Scatter over the breadcrumbs and sprinkle over the Parmesan. Put under the grill for 5 minutes, or until turning golden brown and crisping up.

SERVES 4
Prep time 10 minutes
Cook time about 50 minutes

300g (10¹/₂oz) dried toor dhal
   (yellow lentils/yellow split peas),
   washed in several changes of water
1 tsp ground turmeric
2 black cardamom pods (optional)
3 tbsp vegetable oil
2 cinnamon sticks
4 green cardamom pods
6 cloves
2 tsp black mustard seeds
1 tsp cumin seeds
2 spring onions, finely sliced

2–3 chillies, any colour, deseeded
   if you don't like it fiery, some
   chopped and the rest left whole
2 fat garlic cloves, finely chopped
1 tbsp peeled and finely chopped
   fresh root ginger
6 cherry tomatoes, cut in half
good pinch of salt, or to taste
1 tsp sugar, or to taste
juice of ¹/₂ lemon, or to taste
lots of chopped fresh coriander,
   to garnish

Tadka dhal

*This is probably the most
famous lentil dish coming
out of India – yellow lentils
tempered with spices and the
usual holy trinity of garlic,
ginger and chilli. It has
always been a favourite
of mine and it would grace
our family dinner table at
least once a week when I was
growing up. There are lots of
different recipes for flavouring
the oil (tadka), so play around
with your spice pantry and see
what you come up with. If you
haven't got half of these spices,
then don't worry; just add a
tablespoon of your favourite
spice paste and it will taste
just as delicious.*

Gently boil the lentils in a large saucepan of cold water (around
1 litre /1³/₄ pints will do) and stir in the turmeric and black
cardamom pods (if using) – this will add a subtle smoky flavour.
Allow to cook for around 45 minutes, or until the lentils have
softened and started to break down. Skim off any foam that sits on
the top and give the lentils a stir every now and again in case they
begin to stick on the bottom. If they boil dry, add more water.

Once the lentils have softened, turn down the heat and make the
tadka. Gently heat the oil in a frying pan and add the cinnamon
sticks, green cardamom pods and cloves. When the cardamoms
have turned white and the heads of the cloves have swollen, you
are ready to stir in the mustard and cumin seeds. When they are
sizzling, stir in the spring onions, chillies, garlic and ginger.

After a minute, stir through the tomatoes and turn off the heat.
Pour the tadka into the dhal so that it floats on top. This is the
traditional way to serve it, with the scented oil sitting on top, but
I prefer to stir it through. Season with salt, sugar and lemon juice.
Finally, stir through plenty of chopped fresh coriander and serve
with some rice or fresh bread for the ultimate comfort food.

MAKES 6 REGULAR-
SIZED OR 10 SMALL
Prep time 3 hours, including proving
Cook time 5 minutes per batch

· MY SECRET ·
The secret to
achieving an authentic
result is to get your oven
crazy hot, and I mean
super super hot, as
hot as it will go!

150ml (¼ pint) milk
really good pinch of saffron threads
    – depending on the quality, you
    may need more rather than less
500g (1lb 2oz) plain flour, plus extra
    for dusting
1 tsp baking powder
good pinch of bicarbonate of soda

pinch of salt
1 large egg, lightly beaten
100ml (3½ fl oz) natural yogurt
6 tbsp clear honey
vegetable or rapeseed oil, for
    greasing and drizzling
melted butter or ghee (clarified
    butter), for brushing (optional)

Saffron & honey naan breads

*Naan bread is something I
grew up with. Dad would
bring home all sorts of
interesting flavours from work
to test out. Some were great,
and some not so. Dad would
absorb every remark my
brothers and I would pass over
the table and even ask us how
we felt about new ideas. I've
had too many naans baked in
regular ovens that are so far
away from the traditional
ones made in a classic tandoor
that it put me off making them
myself. But I wanted to nail
this and thankfully, after
much experimentation, I came
up with this wonderful recipe.
Trust me when I say that it's
pretty much like the real naan
breads baked in a searingly
hot clay oven. I've added
saffron and honey for a little
sweetness, but leave them out
if you want them plain (you
needn't heat the milk either).*

Infuse the milk with the saffron by gently heating them together
in a small saucepan. Once the milk has turned golden, turn off
the heat and weigh out the dry ingredients. Mix the flour with
the baking powder, bircarbonate of soda and salt.

In another bowl, whisk together the cooled infused milk,
beaten egg, yogurt and 5 tablespoons of the honey.

Make a well in the dry ingredients and pour in three-quarters of
the wet mixture. Mix together, adding in more of the wet mixture
if you need to until the dough comes together.

Knead the dough on a lightly floured work surface for around
5 minutes until soft and pillowy. Pop into a greased bowl, cover with
clingfilm and leave to double in size. This could take anything from
30 minutes up to 2 hours, depending on how warm your kitchen is.

Once risen, knock back the dough and knead for another minute
before dividing into 6 (for regular) or 10 (for small) dough balls.
Leave the balls to rise on a greased baking sheet loosely covered
with clingfilm. After around 30 minutes they should have puffed
up again. In the meantime, preheat your oven to as hot as it will
go, and pop in a large baking sheet to heat up.

Using your hands or a rolling pin, flatten out each dough ball and
drizzle a little oil over both sides. Brush with some of the remaining
honey, carefully lay on the heated baking sheet and place in the top
part of the oven. After 5 minutes the naan should have puffed up
and turned golden brown, a sign that it's ready. Eat hot, brushed
with a little melted butter or ghee if you want to be indulgent.

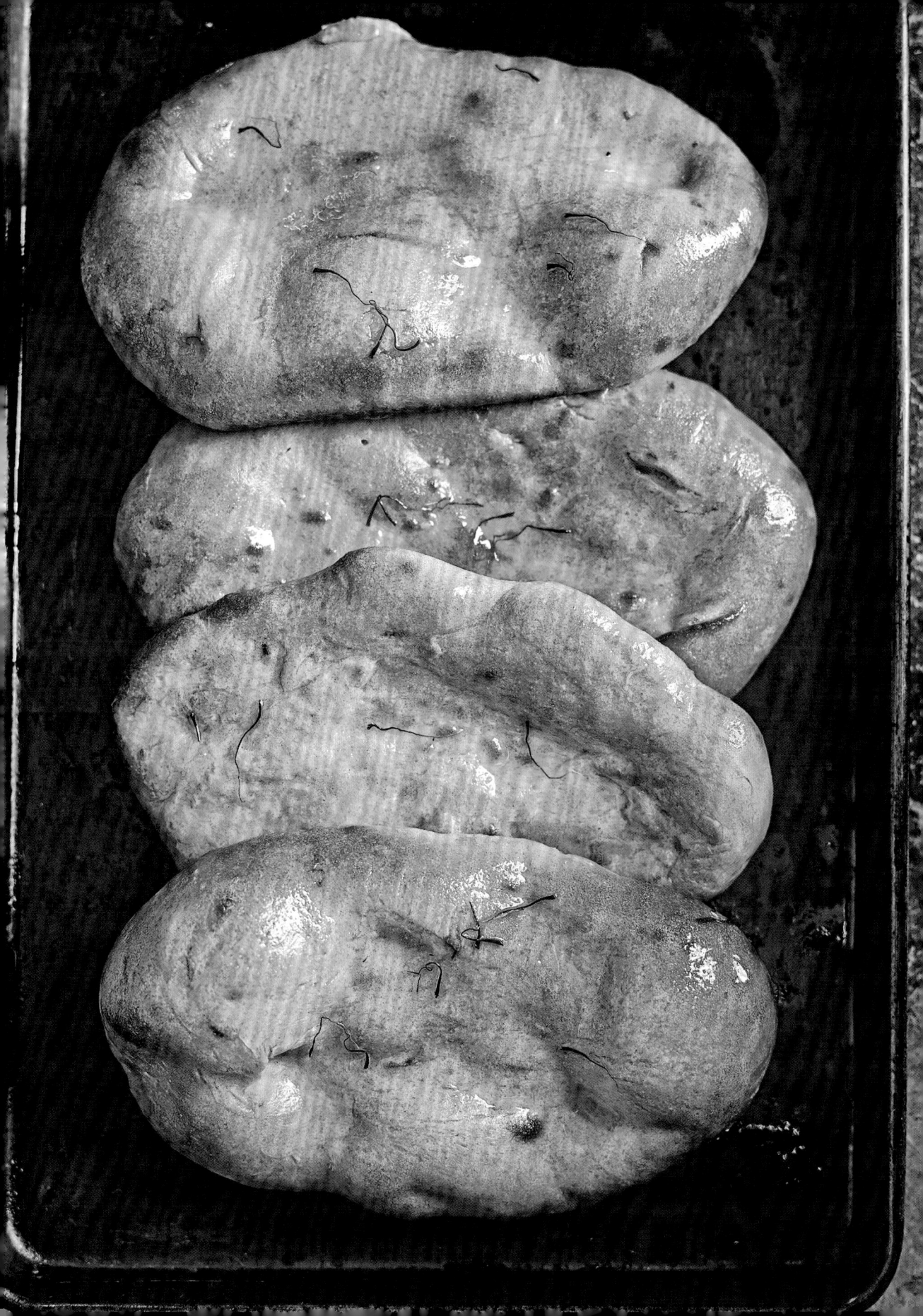

SERVES 4
Prep time 5 minutes
Cook time 5 minutes

400g (14oz) mustard greens,
cut into large bite-sized pieces
1 tbsp oil – I like rapeseed oil or
light olive oil
15g (½oz) butter
2 tsp black mustard seeds

2 spring onions, finely sliced
1 red chilli, deseeded and
finely sliced
2 garlic cloves, finely sliced
good pinch of salt and pepper

Wilted mustard greens (pictured)

I love greens. This recipe has become a firm favourite, as the flavours liven up even the most boring vegetables. I particularly like the deep earthy flavour of mustard greens, but you can use any greens you like. The central core in some of the outer leaves can be rather woody, so just cut it out.

Blanch the mustard greens by cooking them in a large saucepan of boiling water for a few minutes. Then drain and run them under cold water to keep their colour. Drain well again.

Gently heat the oil and butter in a large frying pan and stir in the remaining ingredients. Once the mustard seeds start to sizzle, add the mustard greens and cook for a few minutes until steaming and wilted.

SERVES 4
Prep time 5 minutes
Cook time 25 minutes

1 celeriac, about 800g (1lb 12oz)
1.2 litres (2 pints) milk, or just
enough to cover when boiling
good pinch of saffron threads
4 green cardamom pods, bruised
with a pestle and mortar

4 black peppercorns
2 bay leaves
a few woody thyme sprigs
salt (optional)

Saffron, cardamom & thyme celeriac

Celeriac is one of the unsung heroes of the vegetable family. It is understated, underrated and underused! I love celeriac for its nutty and aromatic flavour, which resembles celery (it's sometimes called celery root) but isn't quite as harsh. You can use celeriac in many different ways, raw or cooked, and it always tastes delicious.

Prepare the celeriac by trimming off the base that contains all the knots and cutting off the hard greenish skin. Roughly chop the rest and put in a saucepan. Pour over the milk so that the celeriac is fully immersed and add the remaining ingredients. Bring to a gentle boil and cook for around 20 minutes until soft and tender.

Strain off the milk and discard the cardamom husks, bay leaves and thyme. Use a fork to mash the celeriac until smooth, or you can use a stick blender if you have one. Taste and add a little salt if you like. Serve as a great alternative to potatoes.

MAKES ABOUT 750G
(1LB 10OZ) OR 1
MEDIUM JAR
Prep time 5 minutes
Cook time 1 hour

100g (3¹/₂oz) red chillies, finely
   chopped – you can remove some
   seeds if you don't want it too fiery
1kg (2lb 4oz) sugar – I prefer white
   granulated sugar
2 tbsp peeled and finely chopped
   fresh root ginger

450ml (16fl oz) white wine vinegar
2 tbsp balsamic vinegar
juice of 1 lime
2 cooking apples, stabbed
   with a knife in a few places

Chilli jam

*This recipe is for all the chilli
lovers out there who simply
must have a little heat in
all their dishes. To make
traditional jam you have to
add a setting agent. Many
fruits contain natural pectin.
This includes cooking apples,
so I have added a few in here
to help the jam set. Although
I'm calling this a jam, it's not
for spreading on your toast,
but more of a relish to have
with cheese or rubbed on
meat as a marinade.*

Gently heat all the ingredients in a heavy-based saucepan and
cook for around an hour, or until the jam has 'set'. It's easy to tell
when jam has 'set'. While it's cooking, pop a small plate in the
fridge or freezer until ice cold. When you think your jam may be
ready, spread a teaspoon of it on to the cold plate and allow it to
cool. Gently push it with your finger. If it wrinkles, then it's set;
if it doesn't, then boil for another 5 minutes before testing it again.

Remove the cooking apples and pour the jam into a sterilized
(*see* My Secret, page 161) medium Kilner jar, or other preserving
jar, while hot. Seal the jar, allow to cool completely, then move
to a cool place. It should keep for around 6 months.

· MY SECRET ·
To save time and your
fingers from burning
when chopping all those
chillies, just blitz the
chillies with the ginger
in a food processor.

MAKES ABOUT 750G
(1LB 10OZ) OR 1
MEDIUM JAR
Prep time 5 minutes
Cook time 50 minutes

1 tbsp olive oil
900g (2lb) red onions, finely sliced
150ml (1/4 pint) balsamic vinegar
150ml (1/4 pint) red wine vinegar
300g (10 1/2oz) light brown sugar
grated rind and juice of 1 lemon
1 tsp ground cinnamon
1 tsp ground mixed spice

Caramelized onion & balsamic chutney

This has to be one of my all-time favourite chutneys. As much as I love the original classic, I fancied livening it up with a few spices, and the end result tasted so wonderful that I wanted to share my recipe with you. Just using balsamic vinegar makes it a little too tart, so I have added the same amount of red wine vinegar too, but you can opt for one or the other if you prefer.

This chutney tastes great with cheese or smeared on top of a juicy burger.

Gently heat the oil in a heavy-based frying pan and fry the onions, moving them around the pan every now and again so that they don't catch and burn. They should have softened after around 20 minutes.

Add the rest of the ingredients and stir well. Allow to cook until the mixture has thickened, which should take around 25–30 minutes.

Pour into a sterilized (*see* My Secret, below) medium Kilner jar, or other preserving jar, while hot. Seal the jar, allow to cool completely, then move to a cool place. It should keep for around 3 months.

· MY SECRET ·
To sterilize your jars, wash them in warm, soapy water and pop in a cold oven set to 150°C/300°F/Gas Mark 2 for 10 minutes to dry out. Carefully fill the hot jars. Alternatively, put them through a quick hot wash in the dishwasher before filling.

SERVES 4 AS A SNACK
Prep time 10 minutes
Cook time 2 minutes

½ tsp kalonji (black onion
    or nigella) seeds
½ tsp cumin seeds
½ tsp fennel seeds
2 crisp green apples,
    such as Granny Smiths
grated rind and juice of
    1 lemon, or to taste

good pinch of sugar, or to taste
pinch of salt, or to taste
300ml (½ pint) natural yogurt –
    you can use low-fat if you like
2 tbsp roughly chopped mint

Green apple relish

There's something about green apples that cleanses your palate instantly. I remember making this recipe a few years ago when I needed something refreshing yet cooling to have with some spicy pork chops. I didn't have any cucumbers rolling around in my fridge, so I looked to the fruit bowl and saw a shiny green apple looking back at me. I added a few pickling spices and this relish has since become one of my favourite dips to have with almost anything.

Lightly toast the spices in a heavy-based frying pan over a gentle heat for a few minutes until fragrant and turning a light golden brown. Pour them into a mortar ready for crushing with a pestle once they have cooled a little.

In the meantime, grate the apples, with the skin, on a cheese grater, making sure you don't grate into the bitter core and seeds. Add the lemon rind and squeeze over the lemon juice to stop the apple colouring, then add a good pinch of sugar and salt before stirring through the yogurt and mint.

Roughly crush the toasted spices and add to the relish. Taste and adjust the seasoning with salt, sugar and lemon juice if you need to.

· MY SECRET ·
This relish works well
as a slaw base – just add
some shredded crunchy
red cabbage and a few
finely chopped spring
onions, and serve with
grilled meats.

SERVES 4 AS A SNACK
Prep time 10 minutes

30 cherry tomatoes (any colour),
seeds removed and roughly
chopped
1 spring onion, roughly chopped
1–2 green chillies, seeds removed
and finely chopped
1 tsp peeled and finely chopped
fresh root ginger

1 tbsp roughly chopped
fresh coriander
good pinch of sugar, or to taste
good pinch of salt, or to taste
good pinch of cracked
black peppercorns

Chunky tomato relish

*This recipe is a version of
a tomato salsa with a little
background heat. It's perfect to
have with poppadums, crisps or
bread. If you like your dips fiery,
then keep the seeds in the chilli.*

Mix all the ingredients together in a bowl, then taste and
add more sugar or salt, depending on how you like it.

SERVES 4 AS A SNACK
Prep time 10 minutes,
plus soaking

1 chipotle chilli, soaked in
warm water for 5 minutes
2 ripe avocados
juice of 1/2 lime
1 spring onion, finely chopped
4 cherry tomatoes, cut in half

1/4 tsp smoked paprika
good pinch of sea salt, or to taste
1 tbsp roughly chopped mint
1 tbsp roughly chopped
fresh coriander

Fiery avo relish

*I discovered smoked paprika
a few years ago and I've been
hooked ever since. I also love
the flavour of chipotle chilli,
which is a smoked jalapeño,
as it really fires dishes up.
It tastes sensational in this
relish, but if you don't have
any, you can just add a regular
chilli. Try serving this with my
Blazing Burgers (see page 114).*

Drain the chipotle chilli, then roughly chop.

Halve the avocados, remove the stones and peel, then smash
the flesh with the back of a fork. Squeeze over the lime juice
and then mix with the remaining ingredients. Taste and adjust
the seasoning if you think it needs it. Serve straight away.

Chunky Tomato Relish

Green Apple Relish

Chilli Jam

Sticky Sweet Date Chutney

Caramelized Onion
& Balsamic Chutney

Fiery Avo Relish

Mango Chutney

Cucumber Raita

Preserved Lemon & Garlic Pickle

SERVES 4
Prep time 5 minutes
Cook time 2 minutes

1 tsp cumin seeds (optional)
1 cucumber
300ml ($^1\!/_2$ pint) natural yogurt –
    you can use low-fat if you like
2 tbsp roughly chopped mint
    or fresh coriander

juice of $^1\!/_2$ lemon
pinch of sugar, or to taste
pinch of salt, or to taste

Cucumber raita

*I think this recipe needs little
introduction. Cucumber raita
is always eaten to cool down
any chilli heat, but sometimes
I like to spice it up and throw
in a chilli or two. There are
plenty of ways to gear up
the flavour, so really play
around with veggies, fruit
and fresh herbs.*

· MY SECRET ·
I love to add roughly
crushed salted peanuts
to this basic raita recipe.
They add a little crunch and
give this classic dip a
whole new dimension.

If using cumin seeds, lightly toast them in a heavy-based frying
pan over a gentle heat for a few minutes until fragrant and turning
a light golden brown. Pour them into a mortar ready for crushing
with a pestle once they have cooled a little.

In the meantime, grate the cucumber, seeds and all, on a cheese
grater. Squeeze out any water before mixing with the yogurt, mint
or coriander and lemon juice. Season with a pinch of sugar and salt.

Roughly crush the toasted cumin seeds (if using) and add to the
raita before tasting and adding more sugar and salt if you like.

Other ideas...
Why not layer up the spices in this dish by heating up a few
tablespoons of vegetable oil and frying off $^1\!/_2$ teaspoon cumin
seeds with 1 teaspoon black mustard seeds, a small handful of
fresh, washed curry leaves and a dried red chilli? Once sizzling,
simply pour over the yogurt mixed with cucumber and season
to taste with salt and pepper.

MAKES AROUND 750G
(1LB 10OZ) OR 1
MEDIUM JAR
Prep time 20 minutes,
plus maturing
Cook time 45 minutes

4 large soft ripe mangoes, around
1kg (2lb 4oz) once you've peeled
and stoned them, chopped into
small bite-sized pieces
500g (1lb 2oz) light brown sugar
1 cinnamon stick
1 tsp kalonji (black onion or
nigella) seeds (optional)

3 dried red chillies, ripped so
that the seeds can fall out
2 tbsp peeled and julienned
fresh root ginger
600ml (1 pint) distilled
malt vinegar
150ml (1/4 pint) bourbon
good pinch of salt

Mango chutney

This popular chutney has
made my family famous all
over the world. This is my
version of the recipe with the
addition of bourbon. It doesn't
overpower the chutney, but
rather adds some depth and
warmth. You can leave the
bourbon out if you wish –
just add more vinegar instead,
but make sure it's distilled
malt vinegar, as regular malt
vinegar is just too strong.

Mix all the ingredients together in a heavy-based saucepan and boil
for around 40–45 minutes. It should thicken and be quite syrupy.

Pour into a sterilized (*see* My Secret, below) medium Kilner jar, or
other preserving jar, while hot. Seal the jar, allow to cool completely,
then move to a cool place and leave for a week. This will give it time
to mature. It should keep for around 3 months.

· MY SECRET ·
Mango chutney is really
versatile. Add a heaped tablespoon
to natural yogurt for a refreshing dip,
use in place of your usual tomato-based
pizza sauce topping (see my Naaza
recipe on page 57) or spread some
on a cheese sandwich – you
won't be disappointed!

MAKES AROUND 1KG
(2LB 4OZ) OR 1
MEDIUM JAR
Prep time 5 minutes
Cook time around 30 minutes

2 tsp cumin seeds
5 dried red chillies or 1 tsp
    dried chilli flakes, depending
    on how hot you like it
800ml (1¹/₃ pints) water
400g (14oz) tamarind
    paste/concentrate

300g (10¹/₂oz) light brown sugar
400g (14oz) pitted dates,
    roughly chopped
good pinch of salt, or to taste

Sticky sweet date chutney

*A good chutney should be
sweet with a little hint of
sourness. This recipe uses
tamarind to add a wonderful
sweet yet sour flavour to the
already sticky sweet dates.*

Lightly toast the cumin seeds and chillies or chilli flakes in a
heavy-based saucepan over a gentle heat for a few minutes until
fragrant and the seeds are turning a light golden brown.

Pour in the water before adding the tamarind, sugar and dates.
Stir well and allow to simmer until the mixture has thickened.
This will take around 20–25 minutes depending on the size
of your pan. Turn off the heat and stir in a good pinch of salt.

Allow to cool until cool enough to taste and adjust the seasoning.
Pour into a hot sterilized (*see* My Secret, page 161) medium Kilner
jar, or other preserving jar. Seal the jar and keep in a cool place
for up to 3 months.

· MY SECRET ·
This recipe tastes
wonderful with smoked
salt. Add a little less than
regular salt, as it is
very strong.

MAKES 1KG
(2LB 4OZ) OR
1 MEDIUM JAR
Prep time 10 minutes, plus
preserving and maturing
Cook time 15 minutes

2 tsp coriander seeds
1 tsp fennel seeds
3 bay leaves
3 dried red chillies
100g (3½oz) sea salt
6 unwaxed lemons
5 tbsp vegetable oil

2 tsp black mustard seeds
2 whole garlic bulbs, cloves
   separated, peeled and sliced
500ml (18fl oz) white wine vinegar
250g (9oz) sugar
1–2 tsp chilli powder

Preserved lemon & garlic pickle

Preserved lemons and garlic pickle are both well-known favourites and taste wonderful, but one day I had a thought – why not combine them and make a pickle that has the best of both? After testing a few versions, I created this amazing recipe that I'm sure you will absolutely love.

Lightly toast the coriander and fennel seeds, bay leaves and chillies in a heavy-based frying pan over a gentle heat for a few minutes until fragrant and the seeds are turning a light golden brown. Mix into the sea salt.

Cut the lemons into quarters, but not all the way through so that they are held together at the base. Tightly pack the salt into the lemons and squeeze into a large clip-top preserving jar (a Kilner jar is perfect for this). Fill the jar with water all the way to the top before sealing closed and leaving to preserve for around a month. Try and be patient and don't open the lid!

When the month is up, strain the salty liquid, keeping the spices and around 100ml (3½fl oz) of the liquid. Wash the lemons under cold running water to remove all the salt and discard any flesh including all the white pith from the inside, leaving only the skin behind. Shred the skin into large slivers.

Gently heat the oil in a saucepan with the mustard seeds and the garlic. When the mustard seeds start to sizzle, toss in the slivers of preserved lemon, vinegar, sugar, chilli powder and reserved salty liquid with the drained spices. Boil for 5–10 minutes, or until the liquid has reduced by half.

Pour into a hot sterilized (*see* My Secret, page 161) medium Kilner jar, or other preserving jar. Seal the jar, allow to cool completely, then move to a cool place and allow to mature for a week. Once opened, this pickle will keep for 3 months.

· MY SECRET ·
If you want your
pickle to have an
authentic Indian slant,
use mustard oil instead
of vegetable oil.

Kitchen shortcuts

Everyone has their own cooking shortcuts: their kitchen secrets to make cooking a breeze. I love opening up my fridge and pantry to discover concoctions and potions I've made that were developed in the hope they would help me in some way. I grew up with a pantry full of shortcuts. There were garam masalas everywhere, some were dry and the rest were wet. Spice pastes are a dream for any cook – see pages 134–5 for some of my faves.

When my grandfather invented spice pastes it wasn't because people didn't have time to cook, it was purely because British cooks didn't know how to cook well with spices. Times have changed and spice pastes have become a storecupboard favourite for even the best cooks as it's easier to grab a jar of paste when you're in a rush, than it is to make your own garam masala, especially seeing as spices taste fresher locked in oil than sitting dry in a pantry. As well as a pantry full of pastes, I always make sure I have some of my own kitchen secrets that I go to time and time again when I need that personal touch.

SCENTED OIL
I love keeping some spiced oils not only for cooking, but also for dipping warm bread into. Some of my favourite flavour combos are listed here:

Chilli & garlic oil
2 fresh red chillies (slit down the middle)
4 large garlic cloves (bashed to release their flavour)
1 sprig of rosemary
300ml (10fl oz) olive oil

Black mustard & dried red chilli oil
2 teaspoons black mustard seeds
5 dried red chillies (ripped in half)
100ml (3½fl oz) mustard oil and 200ml (7fl oz) rapeseed oil, or 300ml (10fl oz) rapeseed oil

Rosemary & black pepper oil
3 sprigs of rosemary
2 teaspoons whole black peppercorns
300ml (10fl oz) olive oil

Turmeric & root ginger oil
5cm (2in) piece fresh turmeric root, peeled and thinly sliced (or 1 teaspoon ground turmeric)
5cm (2in) piece fresh root ginger, peeled and thinly sliced
300ml (10fl oz) rapeseed oil

For each oil, gently heat all ingredients in a large saucepan for 5 minutes. Do not boil. Remove from the heat, allow to cool and transfer to an airtight bottle. Store in a cool, dark place.

TADKAS

A wonderful way to add flavour to lentils and veggies is to infuse spices in a little oil and pour it over the top. You will get a flavour hit with each bite and it's a popular cooking technique in India. Unlike the scented oils that you can keep, tadkas are made at the last minute – have a look at my Tadka Dhal recipe on page 154 for some inspiration of what spices you can use: think aromatics and seeds rather than ground powders. You need to release the aromas and flavour from the spices so gently heat them for a few minutes before turning off the heat. If they burn they will taste very bitter.

READY-MADE MASALAS

Having a few spice blends at the ready is a great way to save time in the kitchen.

Coriander & cumin flavour base

4 tablespoons cumin seeds
2 tablespoons coriander seeds

A simple masala used by most Indian cooks. Simply grind the seeds together then store in an airtight container in a cool, dark place.

Chai masala

I love chai and always make up enough chai masala to last me a few weeks. See my recipe for Heart-warming Chai on page 213 for what spices I use.

Toasted cumin

Lightly toast whole cumin seeds in a dry frying pan for a few minutes, keep them moving to stop them from burning. When they are golden brown and you can smell the aromas, remove from the heat. Allow to cool before grinding as coarse as you like it. Store in an airtight container in a cool, dark place.

Chaat masala

Easy to make, but you can easily buy this well-loved masala from your Asian store. As much as I have harped on about making your masalas fresh, this is one you could buy and not feel bad about. It's tangy, sour and salty flavour will add a 'je ne sais quoi' to your dish. Full of fruity, sour dried mango powder, black salt, cumin, asafoetida, coriander and hints of chilli, once you've tried it you will be hooked and want to sprinkle it on everything.

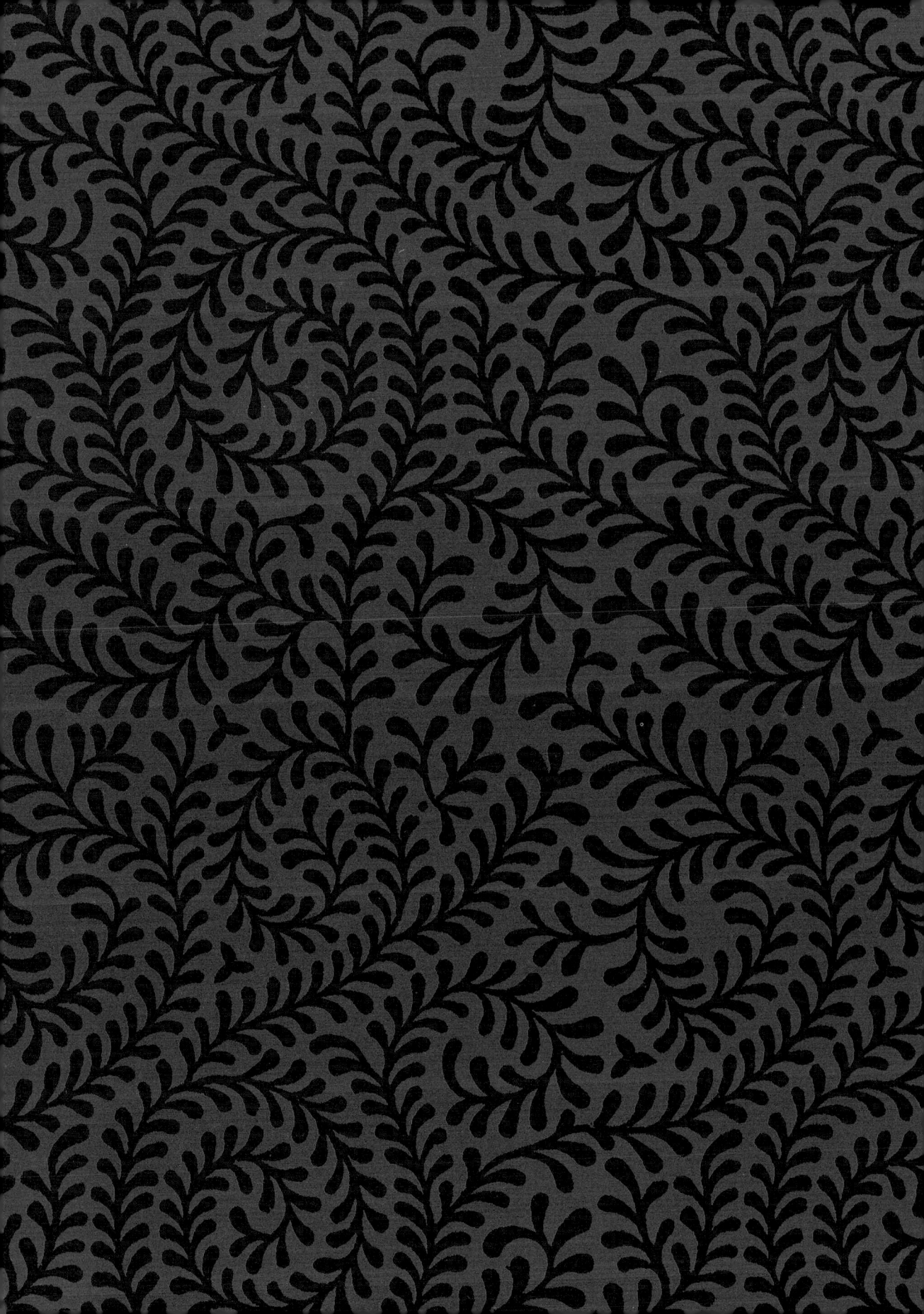

CHAPTER

7

SUGAR &
SPICE

MAKES 8 MINIS
OR 1 LARGE
(SERVES 6–8)
Prep time 10 minutes
Cook time 30 minutes

200g (7oz) sugar
1/4 tsp ground cinnamon
8 green cardamom pods, bruised
with a pestle and mortar
3 Granny Smith apples, peeled,
cored, cut into 1cm (1/2in) thick
wedges and rubbed with the
juice of 1/2 lemon to stop them
from browning

100g (31/2oz) unsalted butter,
chilled and cut into cubes, plus
extra for greasing
300g (101/2oz) shop-bought puff
pastry, rolled out to a few
millimetres thick
freshly grated nutmeg, for sprinkling
ice-cold thick cream or ice cream,
for serving

Baby apple tarte tatin
with spiced caramel

Apple tarte tatin is on my foodie bucket list; it tops my shortlist of best dishes of all time. A year ago a friend of mine set up a supper club where you submit the recipes you would like to have at your last supper. If your menu were to be picked, a supper club would be held in your honour featuring your ultimate menu. Without hesitation this recipe sprung to mind and it will always remain a firm favourite. The most outstanding example I've ever tried was at a Michelin-starred Galvin restaurant in London. I return time after time just for the escargots and the tarte tatin and I can't help but smile every time I visit, as I know what delights are in store for me.

I am using shop-bought puff pastry for this recipe, as it's easier, but feel free to make your own if you like.

Preheat the oven to 200°C/400°F/Gas Mark 6.

Make the caramel by gently heating the sugar with the cinnamon and cardamom in a large frying pan until it melts. (If you are making a large tarte tatin, make sure your frying pan is ovenproof.)

This bit is important. As the sugar melts, it will start to turn golden brown, but don't let it turn too dark or your caramel will be bitter. As soon as it's ready, turn down the heat and carefully beat in the chilled cubed butter. Place the apple wedges in the pan.

Generously grease 8 holes of a muffin (or cupcake) tray with butter. Use a cutter slightly larger than the size of the tray holes to cut out 8 discs from the puff pastry. Prick each pastry disc a few times with a fork. This will stop it puffing up too much in the oven.

Once the apple wedges have been steeping in the caramel for a few minutes, turn off the heat. Carefully spoon the steeped apple wedges into the tray holes, being generous with the caramel but making sure to reserve some for drizzling over later, and then sprinkle over the nutmeg. Top each hole with a pastry disc and tuck in the sides so that the apples are covered and snug in the tin.

Bake for 20 minutes, or until the pastry is golden brown. Remove from the oven and allow to cool for a few minutes before inverting a plate over the tray and turning it all upside down to release the tartes. (You may need to tap the base of the tray to help them out). The pastry should be at the bottom with the sticky, spiced, caramelized apples on top.

Spoon over the reserved caramel and serve with a good dollop of ice-cold thick cream or ice cream. It's heavenly!

SERVES 12
Prep time 15 minutes,
plus freezing

4 eggs
55g (2oz) caster sugar
2 tsp ground green cardamom
500ml (18fl oz) double cream
85g (3oz) roasted hazelnuts, ground,
  plus an extra 15g (¹/₂oz) chopped
200g (7oz) Nutella hazelnut
  chocolate spread

Roast hazelnut & cardamom ice cream

This recipe features three of my favourite ingredients – roast hazelnuts, Nutella hazelnut chocolate spread and the sweet spice cardamom. The ice cream is rather indulgent, as it uses double cream to set it – wonderful if you don't have an ice-cream maker. I love having extra in the freezer as a sweet treat, which is why this recipe is enough for 12 servings.

Get 3 large bowls. Separate the eggs and put the yolks in one bowl and the whites in another, making sure this bowl is particularly squeaky clean (*see* page 196). Add the sugar and cardamom to the yolks, then pour the cream into the third bowl.

Whisk up the whites until you get a stiff peak, preferably using an electric whisk. This means when you lift the whisk out the whites will stand up and stay up.

Whisk the egg yolks until light and pale in colour.

Finally, whisk the cream until it just holds its shape (soft peaks).

Fold the ground hazelnuts into the cream before mixing it into the beaten yolks. Then gently fold in the whites, trying not to knock the air out of them. Stir through the Nutella – I like to swirl it through instead of completely mixing it in. Pour it all into a freezer-proof container, sprinkle over the chopped roasted hazelnuts and pop in the freezer, ideally overnight.

· MY SECRET ·
This tastes great with hot chocolate sauce. Try adding a tablespoon of peanut butter to melting chocolate for some extra nuttiness.

MAKES AROUND
30 MINI MUFFINS
OR 8 LARGE ONES
Prep time 10 minutes
Cook time 15–20 minutes

200g (7oz) plain flour
2 tsp baking powder
$^1/_2$ tsp bicarbonate of soda
2 tsp ground cinnamon
100g (3$^1/_2$oz) dark brown sugar
pinch of salt
65g (2$^1/_2$oz) unsalted butter, melted
 and cooled, plus extra, if not using
 paper cases, for greasing

100ml (3$^1/_2$fl oz) milk
100ml (3$^1/_2$fl oz) buttermilk
1 large egg, whisked

Maple cream
100ml (3$^1/_2$fl oz) double cream or
 whipping cream
3 tbsp maple syrup

Cinnamon mini muffins with maple cream

Muffins are great at any time of the day and they are so simple to make it amazes me that anyone would buy them. I have used buttermilk as well as milk in this recipe, but you can opt for one or the other if you prefer – just make sure you use 200ml (7fl oz) of whichever you choose.

Preheat the oven to 200°C/400°F/Gas Mark 6 and either line 30 holes of mini muffin trays with mini paper cases or grease really well with butter.

Sift the flour, baking powder, bicarbonate of soda and cinnamon together into a bowl. Stir through the sugar and salt, making sure you break up any lumps.

In another bowl, whisk the melted butter, milks and egg together.

Make a well in the centre of the dry mixture and pour in the wet mixture. Fold them together, making sure you don't overmix the batter. Lumps make a lighter muffin!

Fill the paper cases or greased holes with heaped teaspoonfuls of the batter and bake for 15–20 minutes. The muffins should be springy to the touch and an inserted skewer should come out clean when they are cooked.

>>>

· MY SECRET ·
These are perfect to make ahead if you are short on time. Mix the dry ingredients in one bowl and whisk the wet ingredients in another. Pop the wet mix in the fridge. When you are ready, all you have to do is pour the wet mix into the dry, fill your muffin cases and you're ready to bake.

Remove from the tin and leave to cool slightly on a wire rack. In the meantime, make the maple cream by simply whisking the cream with the maple syrup until it forms soft peaks. Serve the muffins next to a generously filled pot of the maple cream.

Other ideas…

I use this recipe as a base for other wonderful flavours, one of my favourites being Pecan Muffins with Saffron Cream.

Pecan muffins with saffron cream

Stir 75g (2³/₄oz) roughly chopped pecan nuts through the dry muffin mixture before mixing in the wet ingredients. Then soak a really good pinch of saffron threads in 1 tablespoon warm milk for a few minutes before whisking it with the cream and maple syrup.

Cinnamon raisin muffins with cardamom cream

Gently heat 75g (2³/₄oz) raisins with enough orange juice to cover in a small saucepan until the raisins are plump. Strain off the juice and add the raisins to the wet muffin mixture. Follow the steps for the cinnamon muffin recipe but add ¹/₂ teaspoon of crushed green cardamom seeds to the maple cream.

Carrot & ginger muffins with maple cream

Add 2 large grated carrots to the dry muffin mix and swap the ground cinnamon for ground ginger. I also love to use all buttermilk for this recipe. Add some orange zest to the cream and whip up with the maple syrup.

SERVES 6–8
Prep time 15 minutes,
plus chilling
Cook time 3 minutes

50g (1³/₄oz) unsalted butter
200g (7oz) ginger biscuits, or use
  digestive biscuits with 1 tsp
  ground ginger
3 chunks of stem ginger in syrup,
  including some of the syrup from
  the jar
300g (10¹/₂oz) cream cheese – I like
  Philadelphia

150g (5¹/₂oz) creamed coconut
  – the ones in blocks or sachets
250ml (9fl oz) double cream
grated rind and juice of 1 lime
  (*see* My Secret, below)
50g (1³/₄oz) coconut flakes or
  desiccated coconut, toasted
  (*see* My Secret, page 182)

Coconut & ginger cheesecake

*I love cheesecakes and have
never been a fan of the New
York-style ones that are baked.
I much prefer the chilled ones,
so here is a recipe that is great
to make ahead and keep
chilled in the fridge until you
need it. Make sure you buy
creamed coconut, available
in blocks or in individual
sachets, and not coconut
cream, as the latter contains
too much coconut water and
your cheesecake won't set.
I've used a springform cake
tin with a loose bottom, which
you shouldn't need to grease
with butter if it's nonstick, but
you can easily prepare these
individually in pretty glasses.*

Gently melt the butter in a saucepan, then pour into a food
processor with the ginger biscuits and stem ginger. Blitz until
combined. Tightly press the crumbs into the base of an 18cm (7in)
round springform, loose-bottomed cake tin and spread out so that
it's an even thickness all over. Pop in the fridge to chill and set while
you make the cheesecake filling.

Beat together the cream cheese, creamed coconut, double cream,
lime juice and around 3 tablespoons of the stem ginger syrup, or
more if you like it sweet. (If you happen to be using crystallized
ginger instead and don't have any syrup, add some icing sugar to
taste.) Spread on top of the ginger crumb base and put back in the
fridge to set for a few hours.

When you are ready to serve, sprinkle the cheesecake all over with
the toasted coconut and lime rind.

· MY SECRET ·
I like to make speedy candied
peel for sprinkling on top of the
cheesecake. Cut pared lime rind into
strips, remove any white pith and heat in
sugar syrup for around 10 minutes.
Carefully (because they will be very hot)
strain the strips, roll them in caster
sugar and allow to cool and crisp up.
Store any extra in an airtight
container for other sweet treats.

MAKES 16 TRUFFLES
Prep time 5 minutes, plus
chilling and warming
Cook time 10 minutes

100g (3½oz) dark chocolate,
   chopped into small pieces
100ml (3½fl oz) double cream
50g (1¾oz) unsalted butter
pinch of salt

Flavourings
dash of orange juice or liqueur, such
   as Amaretto or Tia Maria; a pinch
   of chilli powder (these are optional
   and you needn't stick to only these
   – the sky's the limit!)

Stuffings
nuts; raisins; finely chopped stem
   ginger – goes well with a cocoa
   powder coating

Coatings
finely chopped nuts, such as
   pistachios, hazelnuts or almonds;
   desiccated coconut toasted (*see* My
   Secret, below) or flavoured with
   ground cinnamon or grated
   orange rind; cocoa powder

Decadent chocolate truffles

*Bringing out a plate of
homemade chocolate truffles
at the end of a meal always
gets the 'mmmmm' factor.
This is a simple base recipe
to use and I'm sharing with
you some of my favourite
ingredients that I like to
add to spruce them up. Use
good-quality dark chocolate
with at least 70% cocoa
solids. You can always mix in
a bit of milk chocolate if dark
isn't your thing.*

· MY SECRET ·
It's easy to toast coconut.
Heat dessicated coconut
gently in a dry frying pan,
moving it around often, until
light golden brown. Toasting
coconut releases its lovely
nutty flavour.

Pour boiling water into a saucepan so that it comes a third of the
way up the sides of the pan. Pop a heatproof bowl on top, making
sure the base of it doesn't touch the water, and tip in the chocolate.
Stir it every now and again while it's melting.

In the meantime, gently heat the cream with the butter in another
saucepan until the butter has melted. Don't let the cream boil.

Once the chocolate has melted, remove the bowl from the pan and
pour in the cream mixture. Add the salt – trust me, it brings out even
more flavour in the chocolate – and stir well until the chocolate is
glossy. At this point you can stir in some flavourings, such as orange
juice, a liqueur or even a pinch of chilli powder. Pop in the fridge to
chill and set for at least 2 hours.

Once set, take the truffle mix out of the fridge and allow to warm
up for a few minutes while you get the rest of your flavourings ready.
To make the truffles, simply scoop up a scant tablespoonful of the
chocolate mix and quickly roll it in your hands – you have to be
quick or it will melt. Stuff the truffles if you like and/or roll them in
your chosen coating.

Lay the truffles on nonstick baking paper and pop them in the fridge
until you need them. They will keep for 3 days, if they last that long!

SERVES 4
Prep time 5 minutes
Cook time 8 minutes

150g (5½oz) sugar
grated rind and juice of 2 lemons
1 vanilla pod
5 green cardamom pods
2 star anise
2 cinnamon sticks
4 peaches, cut in half and stones
   removed
150g (5½oz) blueberries
150g (5½oz) blackberries

Saffron crème
4 heaped tbsp crème fraîche or
   natural yogurt
good pinch of saffron threads,
   soaked in 1 tbsp warm water or
   warm milk for a few minutes

Aromatic steeped fruit with saffron crème

This is a recipe for fuss-free days when you fancy something sweet with little effort. By making a simple sugar syrup, you can poach your fruit in minutes. I've chosen peaches, blueberries and blackberries purely because their fantastic colours permeate the syrup, turning it deep crimson, but any soft fruit works here. Serving it with a saffron crème makes this dessert extra special.

Gently heat the sugar and lemon rind and juice in a large frying pan. Split the vanilla pod down the middle lengthways and run the back of the knife down the inside to release the seeds. Add them to the pan with the pod. Bash the cardamoms with a pestle and mortar to release the seeds and then add them all to the sugar syrup with the star anise and cinnamon sticks.

Lay the peaches, cut-side down, in the syrup and toss in the berries. Cook the fruit for 5 minutes, basting with the syrup, before flipping the peaches over and turning off the heat.

Make the saffron crème by mixing the crème fraîche or yogurt with the saffron and its soaking liquid. Serve the aromatic steeped fruit with a good dollop of the saffron crème.

SERVES 4
Prep time 5 minutes,
plus cooling and chilling
Cook time 40 minutes

300ml (1/2 pint) double cream
6 green cardamom pods, bruised
   with a pestle and mortar
8 cloves
1/4 tsp ground cinnamon,
   plus extra for the brûlée top

1 tsp ground ginger
4 egg yolks
3 tbsp light brown sugar,
   plus extra for the brûlée top

Chai brûlée with cinnamon sugar

Crème brûlée is always a crowd pleaser. It is one of my mum's favourite desserts and it's not hard to see why: soft-set creamy custard covered in a layer of caramelized sugar. I love the flavours of chai (Indian tea), and so even though I actually haven't added any tea to this recipe at all, I call it Chai Brûlée because I've used the typical chai spices.

Preheat the oven to 150°C/300°F/Gas Mark 2.

Gently heat the cream, cardamoms, cloves, cinnamon and ginger in a saucepan. When little bubbles start to form around the sides, turn off the heat. Do not let the mixture boil.

In the meantime, whisk the egg yolks with the sugar in a bowl until pale. Pour the spiced cream over and quickly whisk together to make the custard.

Stand 4 individual ramekins in a deep-lipped baking tray. Strain the custard and divide it between the ramekins. Carefully fill the baking tray with boiling water so that it comes halfway up the outsides of the ramekins. I find it easier to do this when I have transferred the tray to the oven.

Bake for 30 minutes before removing the ramekins from the baking tray and leaving to cool to room temperature. Then pop in the fridge to really chill down. There should still be a wobble in the centre.

When completely cold, sprinkle with a little more cinnamon and sugar so that there is an even layer on top of each chai brûlée. Use a kitchen blowtorch or pop under a preheated high grill until the topping is caramelized.

MAKES 12 PARCELS
Prep time 15 minutes
Cook time 12–15 minutes

24 sheets filo pastry, cut into
    rectangles 8 x 18cm (3^1/4 x 7in)
50g (1^3/40z) unsalted butter, melted
50g (1^3/40z) shelled pistachio nuts,
    finely chopped
1 tbsp icing sugar
60g (2^1/40z) chocolate (I prefer
    dark), chopped into small pieces

Sweet tahini dip
2 tbsp tahini
2 tbsp milk
1 tbsp golden syrup

Pistachio & chocolate filo parcels with sweet tahini dip

I grew up having my grandmother's samosas. They were never sweet, always savoury, and like any proud grandmother she would make her own pastry. You can think of this recipe as a sweet samosa stuffed with chocolate and layered with pistachios. There is nothing wrong with using shop-bought pastry; this recipe calls for filo, and the paper-thin sheets turn beautifully crispy in the oven. Making the parcels is a little tricky at first, but once you get the hang of it, it's a breeze.

Preheat the oven to 180°C/350°F/Gas Mark 4 and line a baking sheet with nonstick baking paper.

Lay out a sheet of filo and brush it lightly with melted butter. Sprinkle over some pistachios and a good pinch of icing sugar. Lay another sheet of filo on top. Have the long side of the rectangle facing you. Place a few pieces of chocolate a few centimetres (one inch) in from the left-hand side, in the middle. Fold the bottom left-hand corner of the pastry up to the top of the pastry sheet to form a triangle, then fold the triangle to the right by flipping the left corner over to the right. There will be a big flap of pastry on the right. Brush it with more butter and sprinkle it with nuts and icing sugar. Fold the top left point of the triangle down to the bottom and fold the flap over, encasing the chocolate. Brush the parcel all over with melted butter and lay on the lined baking sheet. Make the rest of the parcels in the same way.

Pop in the oven to cook through for 12–15 minutes, or until golden brown. You may need to flip the parcels over halfway through.

In the meantime, mix the sweet tahini dip ingredients together in a small bowl.

Once the parcels are ready, let cool for 5 minutes before piling high on a platter with the sweet tahini dip on the side.

· MY SECRET ·

Tahini is sesame seed paste and can be found in most supermarkets. If it's not available, or for a change, you can use peanut butter instead. Just add less golden syrup and enough milk to make it thick and creamy.

SERVES 8
Prep time 10 minutes,
plus chilling

300ml (1/2 pint) full-fat natural
   Greek yogurt
200g (7oz) ricotta cheese
1 tsp ground cinnamon
200ml (7fl oz) pomegranate juice
50ml (2fl oz) pomegranate molasses
4–5 tbsp grenadine or clear honey,
   to taste (optional)
seeds of 1 pomegranate, to decorate

Pomegranate & ricotta frozen yogurt

Frozen yogurt has to be one of the best recipes invented. I also just love the combination of pomegranate and yogurt – and here I'm using both pomegranate molasses and pomegranate juice. You can buy pomegranate molasses in most supermarkets, but if you can't find it, then simply leave it out. The colour of this frozen yogurt is stunning if you add grenadine, a syrup that was originally made from pomegranates, although nowadays other berries are added. It doesn't matter which one you use as long as it's free from artificial colours.

Using a blender or food processor, whizz the yogurt and ricotta together until smooth. Toss in the cinnamon, pomegranate juice and pomegranate molasses and mix well. If using, add the grenadine a tablespoon at a time until the mixture is vibrant pink. If you aren't using grenadine, then you may want to add some honey to make the yogurt sweeter. Remember that some of the sweetness will be lost once it's frozen.

Pour the mixture into a freezer-proof container and freeze for about 2 hours until almost frozen. Then whizz it up again in your blender or food processor, or use a stick blender if you have one, to break up any ice crystals that will have formed. Return the mixture to the freezer. Do this at least 3 times, at 2-hour intervals, to remove any ice crystals. Then freeze for a few hours more to really firm up.

When ready to serve, leave the frozen yogurt out of the freezer for around 10 minutes before scooping and sprinkling with the pomegranate seeds.

· MY SECRET ·
Frozen yogurt is usually made with natural yogurt alone, but by adding ricotta, it freezes much better, as yogurt forms a lot of ice crystals unless you use an ice-cream maker. So my recipe doesn't need an ice-cream maker and is a breeze to prepare!

Mum and I at our first home in
Newton-le-Willows, Wigan. Partners
in crime from the word go!

A mini me, of course!

Baa at Nayan's wedding.

One of our classic family holiday shots from a
Caribbean cruise (my parents loved cruising!). Me
looking good as gold (front right) with my brothers
Neeraj (front centre) and Nayan (front left); Mum
and Dad (back left), and Bapuji and Baa (back right).

When Mum and I (left) started working together we realised how much we had in common. She loved passing the baton (or in our case the rolling pin!) onto me and we wrote a cookbook together to celebrate 50 years of Patak's. Getting to work and learn with my Mum will be something I remember forever.

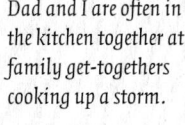

Dad and I are often in the kitchen together at family get-togethers cooking up a storm.

A classic Christmas sight (above): Mum taste-testing the sauce for Dad's ribs. Dad loves making his special ribs for us at Christmas (as much as we love eating them – they are soooooo good). That he is vegetarian makes us appreciate them even more.

Me and my fabulous Leiths girlies (left to right – Beata, Amparo, Mel and Laura). Wine and cheese nights are one of our favourite ways to catch up. This was my turn to host at my apartment in London.

Me on a promo shoot. I am so happy and proud to be part of Baa and Bapuji's continuing legacy while forging a food route of my own.

SERVES 4
Prep time 10 minutes
Cook time 10 minutes

6 ripe peaches, plums and
   nectarines (or any stone fruit),
   cut in half and stones removed
8 green cardamom pods
4 cloves
1/2 tsp ground cinnamon
2 tbsp raisins
2 tbsp clear honey, plus extra
   (optional) for drizzling

Pistachio cream
6 tbsp natural yogurt, or thick
   cream if you want to add
   some indulgence
30g (1oz) shelled pistachio
   nuts, roughly chopped
grated rind of 1 lemon
a little clear honey (optional)

Roast stone fruit & honey with pistachio cream

As a lover of desserts, I'm always looking for quick sugar fixes, which is why I came up with this recipe. I love having friends over for dinner and so I created this fuss-free dish to make my prep easier. It takes just minutes to put together and then all you need to do is pop it in the oven for 10 minutes. It's that simple!

· MY SECRET ·
I love to sprinkle over
some crushed ginger
biscuits just before serving
to add some extra crunch.
It's not sophisticated but
it tastes great!

Preheat the oven to 180°C/350°F/Gas Mark 4 and line a baking sheet with foil.

Lay the stone fruit, cut-side up, on the lined baking sheet. Bash the cardamom pods and cloves together with a pestle and mortar to release their aromatic flavours. You can discard the cardamom husks if you like, but I prefer to leave mine in. Sprinkle over the stone fruit with the cinnamon. Add some raisins to the hollows where the stones were and drizzle over the honey.

Roast for 10 minutes, or until the flesh of the fruit has softened. But don't leave them in too long, as they can quickly collapse and go mushy.

In the meantime, make the pistachio cream by mixing the yogurt or cream with most of the pistachios and most of the lemon rind. Taste and add a little honey if you need to, remembering that the stone fruit is naturally sweet – you can always drizzle it over at the end if you aren't sure.

Allow the roast fruit to cool a little. Spoon over a good dollop of pistachio cream and serve sprinkled with the remaining pistachios and lemon rind, drizzled with a little extra honey if you like.

SERVES 6–8
Prep time 15 minutes
Cook time 1½ hours,
plus cooling

2 egg whites
100g (3½oz) caster sugar –
I like golden caster sugar
2 tsp strong coffee – simply
mix 2 tsp coffee granules
with 1 tbsp boiling water

Spiced cream
175ml (6fl oz) double
or whipping cream
½ tsp ground cinnamon
good pinch of ground
green cardamom
pinch of freshly grated
nutmeg (optional)

grated chocolate, to decorate

Spiced latte meringue

When I was training to be a chef we had special creative days every now and again. After learning all about the different types of meringue (and there are quite a few methods), we were all asked to come up with an idea for a creative meringue day. Ever since then I've been hooked on meringues and I adore them. They are easy to make, but there are a few rules to follow to ensure that they work every time. Make sure all your equipment (bowls, whisk, spoons and so on) is scrupulously clean – the whites won't whisk up properly if they aren't. Use room temperature eggs and, lastly, do please allow the meringues to cool completely before diving in.

This is one of my favourite recipes, using rich coffee and sweet spices. Making a simple coffee meringue means you can add any of your favourite spices to the cream topping. Every mouthful screams Spiced Latte.

Preheat the oven to 120°C/250°F/Gas Mark ½ and line a large baking sheet with nonstick baking paper.

Whisk up the egg whites in a very clean large bowl until you get a stiff peak and they have quadrupled in size. I find it easier to do this with an electric whisk. Keep whisking and add the sugar 1 tablespoon at a time. It will turn glossy and shiny. Fold in the coffee – I like to lightly fold it in to create a marbled effect.

Pour the meringue into the middle of the lined baking sheet and spread it evenly into a circle. Don't worry if there are peaks on top and it's not completely smooth, as that's half the charm of meringues. Bake for 1½ hours. You will know it's cooked as the paper will come away easily from the base and the meringue will be dry. Allow to cool while you make the spiced cream.

Place the cream in a large bowl and sprinkle in the spices. Whip up until it just holds its shape (soft peaks). Keep the cream chilled until you need it.

Once the meringue has completely cooled, top with the spiced cream and sprinkle over some grated chocolate to decorate.

· MY SECRET ·
To make individual meringues, dollop even-sized amounts of the meringue mixture on to the lined baking sheet, then flatten them a little. Bake for about an hour, depending on the size and depth of your meringues.

SERVES 4
Prep time 10 minutes
Cook time 15 minutes

200g (7oz) white long-grain rice
(I like basmati), washed in several
changes of water and left to soak in
cold water for around 30 minutes
if you have time
1 tsp ground green cardamom
4 tbsp brown sugar
grated rind and juice of 2 limes
1 cinnamon stick

2 star anise
1 pineapple, peeled and eyes
removed, cut into 8 slices with
the stringy central core removed
400ml (14fl oz) coconut milk
50g (1³/₄oz) creamed coconut
or 2 tbsp desiccated coconut
25g (1oz) unsalted butter,
chilled and cut into cubes

Coconut cardamom rice pudding with caramelized pineapple

Rice pudding was a favourite school dessert when I was growing up, but although my school meals were good, this was never made well. It's not that hard to get right, especially if you add a few spices along the way. If you can't lay your hands on fresh whole pineapple, then use canned – just strain off as much juice as possible so that it can soak up the caramel.

Bring a saucepan of cold water – about 600ml (1 pint) should do – to the boil. Drain the rice, add it to the water with the cardamom and allow to cook for about 8–10 minutes, or until just soft.

In the meantime, heat a griddle pan over a fairly high heat. Begin the caramel by gently heating half the sugar in a saucepan with the lime juice. Add the cinnamon stick and star anise. After a few minutes the sugar will have melted. Remove the saucepan from the heat and carefully brush some of the melted sugar over the pineapple slices. Put the slices in the hot griddle pan to caramelize, turning them often and basting with any caramel that gathers in the grooves of the pan.

Once the rice is cooked, strain and put in a saucepan with the coconut milk, remaining sugar and creamed or desiccated coconut. Allow to warm through, making sure you stir it often, as it will stick to the base of the pan.

Finish off the caramel by returning the saucepan of melted sugar to a low heat and stirring in the butter until melted and golden.

Serve the rice pudding with the caramelized pineapple drizzled with the caramel. Sprinkle with the lime rind for that added zing (or some candied peel, *see* My Secret, page 180).

SERVES 4
Prep time 10 minutes
Cook time 45 minutes

4 apples (I like Braeburn), peeled, cored and cut into large bite-sized pieces
400g (14oz) seasonal berries, fresh or frozen
2 tbsp peeled and finely chopped or grated fresh root ginger
grated rind and juice of 1 orange

6 tbsp brown sugar
75g (2³/₄oz) unsalted butter, chilled and cut into small cubes
150g (5¹/₂oz) plain flour
1 tsp ground cinnamon
50g (1³/₄oz) roasted hazelnuts, chopped

Sweet cinnamon crumble

Fruit crumble is the ultimate comfort food and fond memories come flooding back every time I eat it. All too often there is never enough fruit and the crumble isn't crunchy enough, so I've remedied that with my recipe for a sweet crumble that is utterly loaded with sweet sticky fruit topped with lots of crunchy nutty crumble. If you use seasonal fruit, you shouldn't need to add more sugar, so give them a taste to check that they are naturally sweet.

Preheat the oven to 200°C/400°F/Gas Mark 6.

Mix all the fruit with the ginger, orange rind and juice and half the sugar in an ovenproof dish.

Make the crumble topping by rubbing the butter into the flour using your fingertips until it resembles breadcrumbs. Stir in the cinnamon, hazelnuts and the remaining sugar. Sprinkle it evenly over the fruit and pop in the oven for 45 minutes.

I'm not a fan of custard, so I serve mine with ice-cold cream or ice cream, but do as you please.

CHAPTER

8

COCKTAIL
TIME

SERVES 4
Prep time 5 minutes

600ml (1 pint) thick natural yogurt – you can use low-fat if you prefer
600ml (1 pint) chilled water, or have a few ice cubes at the ready
really good pinch of salt (for salty lassi) or sugar (for sweet lassi), or to taste

good pinch of toasted cumin seeds (*see* page 171), roughly crushed with a pestle and mortar, or to taste, plus extra to serve

Creamy, salty & sweet lassi

Lassi is the cooling yogurt drink served with many Indian meals. The best lassi I ever had was on the streets of Amritsar in the Punjab, which is famous for this rich and creamy drink. They freshly churn homemade curd using the traditional old-fashioned tools until frothy, before pouring it from a height into tall glasses. It's then topped with a huge scoop of fresh cream from the top of the curd, making it a meal in itself – luxuriously rich and too yummy for words.

You can find both salty and sweet lassis, and I prefer the former. I grew up with fresh lassi made with a masala (see recipe opposite) – sometimes just toasted cumin, other times even more special with whole cloves, fresh curry leaves and fresh coriander.

Whisk together the yogurt and water (and ice if you need it) until frothy and bubbly. Add the salt or sugar and toasted cumin and whisk again.

Taste and adjust the flavour with salt or sugar, if you need to, before pouring into 4 tall glasses. Sprinkle over a little more toasted cumin before serving.

· MY SECRET ·
Try adding a flavoured salt such as lavender salt, fleur de sel or rock salt. It will add depth to the taste and in some cases a little colour.

SERVES 4
Prep time 5 minutes

500ml (18fl oz) thick natural yogurt
– you can use low-fat if you prefer
600ml (1 pint) chilled water, or have
a few ice cubes at the ready
6 tbsp prepared ripe fruit, such as
mango pulp, mashed strawberries
or puréed berries

good pinch of green cardamom
seeds, crushed with a pestle and
mortar, or ground cinnamon,
plus extra to serve (optional)
pinch of sugar, to taste (optional)

Sweet fruity lassi

*Sweet lassis are made using
puréed fresh fruit with the
occasional addition of sweet
spices. In Pakistan they
sometimes add saffron,
which tastes divine.*

Whisk together the yogurt and water (and ice if you need it)
until frothy and bubbly. Stir in the fruit and whisk again.

Taste and adjust the flavour with the spices (if using) and sugar,
if you need to. Pour into 4 tall glasses and sprinkle over a little
more spice (if using) before serving.

SERVES 4
Prep time 5 minutes
Cook time 3 minutes

600ml (1 pint) thick natural yogurt
– you can use low-fat if you prefer
600ml (1 pint) chilled water, or have
a few ice cubes at the ready
2 tbsp vegetable oil – you can use
ghee if you prefer
a few cloves

1 tsp cumin seeds
around 10 fresh curry leaves
(*see* My Secret, page 20)
1 green chilli, slit down the
middle but left whole
a few tbsp chopped fresh coriander
salt

Salty masala lassi

*To make a salty masala lassi
like the one I grew up with,
you need to temper some
spices before pouring into
the whisked yogurt.*

Whisk together the yogurt and water (and ice if you need it)
until frothy and bubbly.

Gently heat the oil (traditionally it would be made using ghee)
in a heavy-based frying pan and add the spices, curry leaves and
chilli. Once they are sizzling, carefully pour into the frothy yogurt
mix, including the chilli, and add salt to taste.

Stir the fresh coriander through the lassi and pour into 4 tall
glasses to serve.

SERVES 6
Prep time 2 minutes

6 tbsp pomegranate juice
small handful of pomegranate seeds
75cl bottle chilled Prosecco

Pomegranate bellini

Although bellinis are
traditionally made with
peach, I prefer to make
mine with jewel-coloured
pomegranate.

Add 1 tablespoon pomegranate juice to each of your
glasses and toss in a few pomegranate seeds.

Top up with chilled Prosecco.

SERVES 6
Prep time 2 minutes

4 tbsp blood orange juice
dash of orange blossom water
75cl bottle chilled Prosecco
strips of orange rind, to garnish (optional)

Orange blossom bellini

The combination of orange
blossom and blood orange juice
is incredible, and even better
when mixed with Prosecco.
You can find orange blossom
water in the baking aisle of
the supermarket, but go easy
with it, as it's strong. This is
a fantastic start to any meal.

Mix the orange juice with the orange blossom water
and divide between 6 glasses.

Top up with chilled Prosecco and garnish with a twist
of orange rind if you like.

· MY SECRET ·
If you want your bellinis
dressed to impress, add a
cinnamon stick to each
glass before topping
up with Prosecco.

OPPOSITE PAGE:
Left: Salty masala lassi
Centre: Pomegranate bellini
Right: Orange blossom bellini

SERVES 4
Prep time 2–5 minutes

3cm (1¼in) piece fresh root
   ginger, peeled and thickly sliced
500ml (18fl oz) cranberry juice
grated rind and juice of ½ lime
4 cinnamon sticks, to serve
lots of crushed ice
600ml (1 pint) chilled
   sparkling water

Crimson ginger sparkler

*This is an alcohol-free cocktail
full of fresh cranberry and lime
juice and warming ginger
and cinnamon.*

Bash the ginger slices with a pestle and mortar to release
some of their juice.

Mix the ginger with the cranberry juice, lime juice, cinnamon
sticks and some crushed ice to infuse the flavours. Strain if
you wish (reserving the cinnamon sticks) or pour directly
into 4 tumblers filled with more crushed ice.

Top up with the sparkling water and sprinkle over the lime
rind. Place a cinnamon stick in each glass and serve.

SERVES 4
Prep time 2–5 minutes

200ml (7fl oz) lychee juice
400ml (14fl oz) apple juice
good pinch of freshly grated nutmeg
lots of crushed ice
400ml (14fl oz) chilled
   sparkling water
apple slices, to garnish (optional)

Lychee, apple & nutmeg crush

*The flavours in this mocktail
scream dessert. Apples and
nutmeg are a match made in
heaven, and when you throw
lychees into the mix, you've got
yourself one amazing drink.*

Mix all the ingredients except the sparkling water together.

Pour into 4 tumblers, top up with the sparkling water and
garnish with apple slices if using.

OPPOSITE PAGE:
*Left: Lychee, apple & nutmeg crush
Centre: Malabar espresso martini
Right: Crimson ginger sparkler*

1–2 tbsp maple syrup, or to taste
20 mint leaves, plus extra to garnish
200ml (7fl oz) your favourite rum
2 limes, cut into quarters
lots of crushed ice
400ml (14fl oz) soda water

Maple & lime mojito

This is a wonderful rum cocktail to make if you have a menu filled with spice. This recipe is full of refreshing lime flavour and sweet maple syrup, with a little cooling mint in the background.

Tip the maple syrup and mint leaves into a bowl or cocktail shaker and bash together until the leaves are broken and you can smell the fresh flavours of the mint. Add the rum and squeeze in the juice from the lime quarters. Toss in the lime quarters and a little crushed ice and mix together.

Fill 4 tumblers with more crushed ice and strain the mojito mix into the glasses. Top up with the soda water, taste and add a little more maple syrup if you like your mojitos sweet. Garnish with a few extra mint leaves.

SERVES 4
Prep time 5 minutes
Cook time 6 minutes

600ml (1 pint) water
4 tsp fresh tea leaves or 4 tea bags –
   I like Darjeeling but any will do
8 cloves
8 green cardamom pods
1/2 tsp fennel seeds

1/2 tsp black peppercorns
1 tsp peeled and grated fresh
   root ginger
handful of mint leaves (optional)
600ml (1 pint) milk
sugar, to taste (optional)

Heart-warming chai

*I fell in love with chai
from the moment I tried its
heavenly sweet flavour. Chai
is ubiquitous in India, and
each spice blend is slightly
different. It's always full of
flavour and usually overly
sweet. I like to add sugar to
taste, as the spices sweeten up
the tea a little and so you may
not even need to add any. Like
most families, I grew up with
our very own secret masala
chai spice blend. The secret
was always closely guarded
and only ever passed down to
a worthy recipient when the
time was right. There are many
good ready-made chai masalas
you can buy, but there is really
nothing like adding fresh spices
to your bubbling tea leaves
to create the perfect heart-
warming chai.*

Pour the water into a large saucepan, add the tea and turn the
heat on. Gently crush the cloves, cardamoms, fennel seeds and
peppercorns with a pestle and mortar. Stir into the pan with the
ginger and mint (if using) and bring the water to a rolling boil.

Once the water is boiling, pour the milk into the tea and bring
to the boil, then turn off the heat. Taste and add sugar if you like.
Strain the tea and serve piping hot.

· MY SECRET ·
My grandmother used
to add fresh mint leaves
to the water while it was being
infused with tea and spices.
It makes the chai taste
remarkably refreshing,
and so I now always add
them to mine.

Wine & spice

Choosing what to drink with spicy food can be a minefield. With this is mind, a few years ago I decided to take the gold standard of wine qualifications and studied the Wine and Spirit Education Trust advanced module in London. Two weeks full time at wine school sounds like a dream, but it was a lot harder than it sounds and although I tasted some incredible wines I soon learnt that the world of wine is absolutely huge and always changing.

If you are like me and prefer to drink wine with an Indian meal, then it's useful to know what style of wine will complement your dish. I don't propose to be a wine expert, far from it, so think of this as a rough guide to different wine styles that have been found to work well with spice-infused recipes.

It's good to pick a wine that has a little sweetness and good acidity as most spice recipes have a hint of both. This could be from the tomatoes, lemons, added sugar and even the sweet nature of some spices. Try to avoid oak and high alcohol wines, as this will accentuate the heat in the dish. I prefer red wines that are lighter in style as heavy tannic wines can make your food taste bitter, but do please your own palate. Wine is subjective and it's better to choose one you like rather than to drink one because someone said it works.

There is no one wine that fits all so think about what spices you are using, how much chilli you've added, and how heavy the sauce is (if any). In some cuisines the protein is the star of the dish and the wine should match it accordingly, but with Asian food this isn't the case. If your protein is laced with spice or coated in sauce, you need something to balance these elements instead.

There are so many good wine styles, as well as excellent sparkling wines and champagnes, that match with spice-driven dishes, so don't be shy to try a few. Here are just a few of my favourites to help you on your way of wine exploration:

White

VOUVRAY

Made in the French Loire Valley from the Chenin Blanc grape, Vouvray's high acidity stands up to flavoured hearty sauces and it typically has flavours of ginger, fig and nuts. It has the potential to age well and can be found in a few different styles – dry, off dry and sweet. Try an off dry Vouvray with a spicy masala full of rich flavours, or a sweet Vouvray with my Tarte Tatin (*see* page 174).

VIOGNIER
This is the name of the grape variety known to produce naturally aromatic wines. Its fruit-driven style means it pairs well with spiced foods, especially the Californian and Australian wines that have hazelnut and stone fruit characteristics. Try with a mild, creamy fish recipe.

GEWURZTRAMINER
This wine has a natural sweetness and the scent and flavour of lychees: 'gewürz' means spicy in German. You can now find good examples of this wine in other parts of the world. Try with spiced, nutty, fruity recipes such as my Roast Aubergine Salad (*see* page 82).

RIESLING
This is a grape that originated in Germany but is now grown all over the world. Where it is grown will influence its taste, but typically it has a good balance of sugar and acidity that means it can handle the flavours from spicy dishes. Try a slightly sweet-tasting German Riesling with a hearty masala with a good level of chilli.

Red

BEAUJOLAIS
Beaujolais is a wine region that uses the Gamay grape. A light-bodied, low tannic wine with low to medium acidity it works wonders with Indian dishes and can taste even better when slightly chilled. It typically has flavours of red berries and has been described as 'the only white wine that happens to be red'. Try with a creamy tomato-based dish with medium chilli levels such as my Chicken Tikka Masala (*see* page 52).

CARMENERE
Originally grown in France, but now more so in Chile, this crimson wine has flavours of cherries and spice with some earthy undertones that make it great with Indian food. Try with my Slow-roast Spiced Lamb (*see* page 44).

SYRAH (SHIRAZ)
This wine has always been a popular choice for its powerful flavours and fuller body. I often find it too heavy and prefer it when it has been blended and so becomes lighter in style and more palatable with heavy flavoured meat dishes. Try with a spicy robust dish such as my Chilli Beef with Black Pepper (*see* page 60).

Index

Biography

Anjali Pathak is an exciting talent in the Indian food and spice arena with a fun-loving and warm character. Having learned the basics of Indian cookery from a young age, Anjali has stepped out of her heritage and works with spice and flavours from across the globe. Not only is she the next generation of a family that brought Indian cuisine to households around the world, Patak's, she has an award-winning cookbook under her name and regularly appears at food festivals.

Anjali is a respected chef, food writer and cookery teacher and has been shortlisted for a number of awards for her work with Indian food and flavours. With qualifications from the prestigious Leiths School of Food and Wine, Wine Spirit and Education Trust (WSET) and a diploma in Diet and Nutrition, Anjali continues to go from strength to strength, regularly appearing on television across the world. Anjali's work has appeared in leading international food and lifestyle media and her cookery masterclasses are always a sell out.

Connect with Anjali online at www.anjalipathak.com or via Twitter and Instagram @anjali_pathak.

Acknowledgements

There are too many people I would like to thank who have helped bring my book to life. I won't ramble on but I need to thank my design team at Smith & Gilmour who have put my pages together with beauty and vibrance, you were a joy to work with and it looks better than I ever imagined. Thanks to my food stylist Aya and my photographer Martin, whom not only shot the most beautiful images but both had some great recipe ideas they were very keen to share! Eleanor, Polly and all the team at Octopus for persevering with me and meticulously going through my manuscript to make sure the book is perfect. I can't begin to tell you how pleased I am with it. To all my wonderful tasters, thank you all for lending me your taste buds.

A very special thank you to my wonderful agent Anne Kibel, who has supported all my wishes and continues to help my food dreams come true.

And finally, a very special thank you to my wonderful family and partner. No matter how crazy my dreams are, you are always by my side and your guidance is something I will never take for granted. You continue to inspire me to set my goals high, and with hard work I hope to make you proud. I wouldn't be who I am today if it weren't for you, so thank you for all you have done for me. I love you with all my heart.

An Hachette UK Company
www.hachette.co.uk

First published in Great Britain in 2015 by Mitchell Beazley
a division of Octopus Publishing Group Ltd
Carmelite House, 50 Victoria Embankment
London EC4Y 0DZ
www.octopusbooks.co.uk

This paperback edition published in 2017

ISBN: 978-1-78472-314-9

A CIP catalogue record for this book is available from
the British Library.

Printed and bound in China.

10 9 8 7 6 5 4 3 2 1

Senior Commissioning Editor: Eleanor Maxfield
Editor: Pollyanna Poulter
Art Director: Jonathan Christie
Design & Art Direction: Smith & Gilmour
Photography: Martin Poole
Food Styling: Aya Nishimura
Prop Stylists: Lydia Brun, Iris Bromet & Linda Berlin
Indexer: Isobel McLean
Production Controller: Sarah Kramer

Standard level spoon measurements are used in all recipes
1 tablespoon = 15 ml spoon
1 teaspoon = 5 ml spoon

Both metric and imperial measurements have been
given in all recipes. Use one set of measurements only,
and not a mixture of both.

Fresh herbs should be used unless otherwise stated.
Pepper should be freshly ground black pepper unless
otherwise stated.

Ovens should be preheated to the specific temperature –
if using a fan-assisted oven, follow manufacturer's
instructions for adjusting the time and the temperature.

Eggs should be medium unless otherwise stated. The
Department of Health advises that eggs should not be
consumed raw. This book contains dishes made with raw
or lightly cooked eggs. It is prudent for more vulnerable
people such as pregnant and nursing mothers, invalids,
the elderly, babies and young children to avoid uncooked
or lightly cooked dishes made with eggs.

This book includes dishes made with nuts and nut
derivatives. It is advisable for people with known allergic
reactions to nuts and nut derivatives or those who may
be potentially vulnerable to these allergies, such as pregnant
and nursing mothers, invalids, the elderly, babies and children,
to avoid dishes made with nuts and nut oils. It is prudent
to check the labels of all pre-prepared ingredients for the
possible inclusion of nut derivatives.

This book contains dishes made with fresh curry leaves and
raw beansprouts. Curry leaves and raw beansprouts should
be thoroughly washed before use and avoided by vulnerable
people such as pregnant and nursing mothers, invalids,
the elderly, babies and young children.

DK findout!

Big Cats

Author: Andrea Mills

Project editor Clare Lloyd
Project art editor Emma Hobson
Senior editor Marie Greenwood
Assistant editors Shalini Agrawal, Shambhavi Thatte
Art editor Shipra Jain
Senior art editor Nidhi Mehra
DTP designers Anita Yadav, Mohammad Rizwan
Picture researcher Sakshi Saluja
Jacket co-ordinator Francesca Young
Jacket designer Kartik Gera
Educational consultant Jacqueline Harris
Managing editors Laura Gilbert, Alka Thakur Hazarika
Managing art editors Diane Peyton Jones,
Romi Chakraborty
Delhi team head Malavika Talukder
Senior pre-production producer Tony Phipps
Senior producer Isabell Schart
Creative director Helen Senior
Publishing director Sarah Larter

First published in Great Britain in 2019 by
Dorling Kindersley Limited
80 Strand, London, WC2R 0RL

Copyright © 2019 Dorling Kindersley Limited
A Penguin Random House Company
10 9 8 7 6 5 4 3 2 1
001–311567–Feb/2019

A CIP catalogue record for this book
is available from the British Library.
ISBN: 978-0-2413-5841-2

Printed and bound in China

A WORLD OF IDEAS:
SEE ALL THERE IS TO KNOW

www.dk.com

Contents

Ocelot

Snow leopard

Caracal

Cheetah

Tigers fighting

Rusty-spotted cat

3

What is a big cat?

The five main big cats are the mightiest members of the cat family. These fierce, furry animals have striking fur, super senses, and powerful bodies suited to high-speed hunting in the wild. They are among the world's best-known mammals and most successful in hunting animals to eat.

Snow leopard

Jaguar

Tail

A long, thick tail helps big cats keep their balance while chasing animals to eat, called prey. The tail also helps cats change direction or climb trees.

Tiger

Claws

A cat's sharp claws are also retractable. This means they can be withdrawn or extended as necessary.

Fur
Patterned coats are the perfect camouflage for big cats. They help them blend in with their surroundings and hide from prey.

Lion

Teeth
Big cats have large and pointed canine teeth. Their back teeth are like scissors. They use these teeth to cut into meat and break it into small chunks that are easy to swallow.

Leopard

Legs
With long and powerful legs, big cats can chase down their prey at breathtaking speeds.

FACT FILE

» **Weight:** 4.5 kg (10 lb)

» **Life expectancy:** up to 18 years

» **Speed:** up to 48 kph (30 mph)

» **Sleep:** up to 16 hours

» **Habitat:** human home

» **Diet:** meat

Balancing act
Pet cats use their tails to balance on the branches of trees, narrow ledges, or fences.

Feline fur
Most pet cats have patterned fur with similar markings to big cats.

Domestic cats

Pet cats are generally smaller than big cats. They are tame, or domesticated, animals who are used to being near people. Many pet cats enjoy the safety of a secure home and regular meals, and love to cuddle up to their owner. However, if pet cats are neglected, they soon turn wild (feral) and learn to look after themselves – just like a big cat!

Pet cat or big cat?

Whether a pet cat or a big cat, all cats, or felines, have similar features. These include big eyes, long whiskers, sharp teeth, and claws that scratch. However, while big cats need to hunt for survival, most domestic cats are used to being fed and cared for by humans.

Playful paws
Retractable claws are most often released to scratch posts, or sometimes to catch mice and birds.

Cat camouflage
A big cat's patterned coat helps it to hide in thick undergrowth and grassland.

Big cats

While a domestic cat may bring home a mouse as a present for its owner, big cats, such as this jaguar, must feed regularly in order to live. Their bodies are built for high-speed chasing and expert hunting. Apart from the sociable lion, most big cats live alone.

Hunter hearing
The ears of big cats are sensitive to even the slightest sound carried over long distances.

! WOW!

The **Ancient Egyptians** first domesticated wild cats for **hunting rats and mice**.

FACT FILE

» **Weight:** 17–310 kg (37–680 lb)

» **Life expectancy:** up to 20 years

» **Speed:** up to 120 kph (74 mph)

» **Sleep:** up to 20 hours

» **Habitat:** forests, mountains, jungles, grasslands, and deserts

» **Diet:** raw meat

Killer claws
Almost all big cats have very sharp, retractable claws to take down and tear into prey.

Meet the big cats

Here are the five main big cats. Apart from the snow leopard, they are the only cats that can roar. They are among the top hunters, or predators, in the habitats they call home. While big cats prey upon smaller and weaker animals in order to stay alive, no other animal needs to hunt big cats for food.

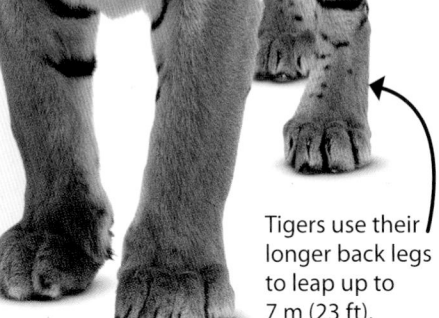

» Scale

Tiger

The biggest and heaviest cat is the tiger. This solitary hunter stalks its prey under cover of darkness. Tigers live in Asia, ranging from India's steamy tropics to Siberia's icy forests.

FACT FILE

» **Length:** 2–3.5 m
(6 ft 6 in–11 ft 6 in)

» **Weight:** up to 318 kg
(700 lb)

» **Continent:** Asia

» **Habitat**: tropical
rainforests and conifer forests

Tigers use their longer back legs to leap up to 7 m (23 ft).

» Scale

Lion

Nicknamed the "king of the jungle", the lion is known for its majestic mane and thunderous roar. Unlike most big cats, lions live in family groups called prides. Here, hunting is a team effort.

FACT FILE

» **Length:** 1.4–2.5 m
(4 ft 7 in–8 ft 2 in)

» **Weight:** up to 250 kg
(420 lb)

» **Continent:** Africa and India

» **Habitat:** grasslands

Leopard

This big cat is an expert climber, spending much of its time high in the trees. Leopards live alone, hunt at night, and can carry their prey up into leafy branches to deter scavengers.

FACT FILE

» **Length:** 1–1.6 m (3 ft 4 in–5 ft 3 in)

» **Weight:** up to 90 kg (200 lb)

» **Continent:** Africa and Asia

» **Habitat:** forests, mountains, deserts, and grasslands

» Scale

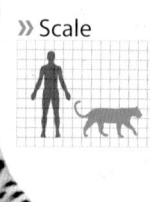

Jaguar

The largest cat in the Americas is the jaguar. Found in wetter regions, this cat is a strong swimmer and targets prey in rivers as well as on land.

FACT FILE

» **Length:** 1–2 m (3 ft 3 in–6 ft 6 in)

» **Weight:** up to 100 kg (220 lb)

» **Continent:** Central and South America

» **Habitat:** forests, marshlands

» Scale

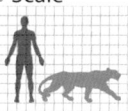

» Scale

Snow leopard

The most secretive big cat is the snow leopard, which lives high in the snowcapped mountains of central Asia. This feline has woolly fur and uses its tail for balance.

FACT FILE

» **Length:** 1.1 m (3 ft 7 in)

» **Weight:** up to 55 kg (120 lb)

» **Continent:** Asia

» **Habitat:** mountains

A snow leopard's furry tail doubles up as a blanket.

Wild cats

Although not as large, wild cats share many of the same physical characteristics as the five big cats. Camouflaged coats help them to stay hidden from the prey they hunt. However, unlike most of the big cats, none of these wild cats can roar.

! WOW!

Talented tree climbers, clouded leopards can **hang upside down** by their back legs!

Clouded leopard

Named "tree tiger" in Malaysia, the clouded leopard is a tree-climbing forest-dweller in Southeast Asia. It is the same size as a small leopard, but has a coat patterned like coloured clouds. This solitary cat hunts deer, monkeys, and pigs.

» Scale

FACT FILE

» **Length:** 0.9 m (2 ft 11 in)

» **Weight:** up to 23 kg (50 lb)

» **Continent:** Asia

» **Habitat:** forests

» **Length:** 1–1.5 m
(3 ft 3 in–4 ft 11 in)

» **Weight:** up to 70 kg
(155 lb)

» **Continent:** Africa

» **Habitat:** grasslands

Cheetah

The fastest animal on land is the cheetah. A long and flexible backbone propels the cheetah to record-breaking speeds across the African grasslands, or savannah.

» Scale

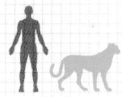

Puma

The first European settlers to the Americas mistook the puma for a lion. The puma is the biggest jumper of all cats, covering 12 m (40 ft) in a single leap.

» Scale

FACT FILE

» **Length:** 2.5 m (8 ft 2 in)

» **Weight:** up to 100 kg
(220 lb)

» **Continent:** North and South America

» **Habitat:** forests and mountains

» Scale

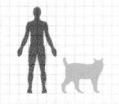

Eurasian lynx

One of Europe's biggest predators, the Eurasian lynx has the power to hunt deer. It also eats smaller prey, including foxes and rabbits.

FACT FILE

» **Length:** 1.3 m (4 ft 3 in)

» **Weight:** up to 30 kg
(66 lb)

» **Continent:** Europe and Asia

» **Habitat:** forests and scrublands

Smaller wild cats

Wild cats can be even smaller than domestic pets. Despite their small size, the patterned fur, lightweight bodies, and soundless movements of these cats make them successful hunters in their habitats, or homes.

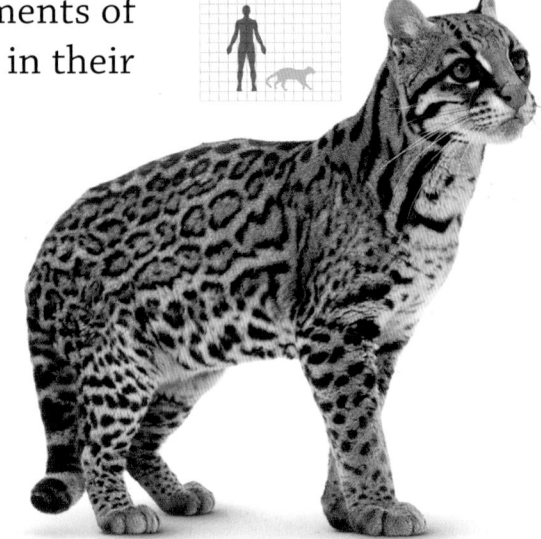

» Scale

Ocelot

This American wild cat is about twice the size of a pet cat. It sleeps in leafy foliage (plants) during the day, and hunts mice and other rodents when it is dark.

FACT FILE

» **Length:** 1 m (3 ft 3 in)

» **Weight:** up to 20 kg (44 lb)

» **Continent:** North and South America

» **Habitat:** forests and grasslands

» Scale

Serval

Long legs and neck allow the spotty serval to see over tall savannah grass. The speedy serval also has large ears and an excellent sense of hearing.

» Scale

FACT FILE

» **Length:** 0.7 m (2 ft 6 in)

» **Weight:** up to 18 kg (40 lb)

» **Continent:** Africa and Asia

» **Habitat:** forests, grasslands, and deserts

Caracal

This small wild cat has long legs and can make giant leaps. It is one of the few cats with large, black-tipped tufty ears.

FACT FILE

» **Length:** 0.8 m (2 ft 7 in)

» **Weight:** up to 18 kg (40 lb)

» **Continent:** Africa

» **Habitat:** grasslands

Bobcat

The most common cat in North America is the bobcat. Unlike other wild cats, this solitary hunter has a very short tail.

» Scale

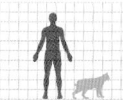

FACT FILE

» **Length:** 0.7 m (2 ft 4 in)

» **Weight:** up to 18 kg (40 lb)

» **Continent:** North America

» **Habitat:** forests, swamps, and deserts

Rusty-spotted cat

The world's smallest wild cat, the rusty-spotted cat, comes from Asia. Smaller than most domestic cats, it weighs about 200 times less than a lion.

» Scale

» Scale

FACT FILE

» **Length:** 0.4 m (1 ft 4 in)

» **Weight:** up to 1.4 kg (3 lb)

» **Continent:** Asia

» **Habitat:** forests and grasslands

Sand cat

This desert dweller escapes the heat by sleeping in a sand burrow during the day, and hunts lizards and mice at night.

FACT FILE

» **Length:** 0.5 m (1 ft 8 in)

» **Weight:** up to 3 kg (6 lb 8 oz)

» **Continent:** Africa and Asia

» **Habitat:** deserts

Fishing cat

This strong swimmer lives in wet regions of Asia. Fishing cats dive into water to catch fish, either in the mouth or between its webbed paws.

» Scale

FACT FILE

» **Length:** 0.8 m (2 ft 7 in)

» **Weight:** up to 9 kg (20 lb)

» **Continent:** Asia

» **Habitat:** forests and wetlands

Spots

A spotty coat provides perfect camouflage in sunny grasslands. The light base colour with darker spots combine to go unnoticed in the long grass. This gives a big cat cover while lying in wait for prey.

Stripes

Tigers are known for their striking, striped fur, but they also have striped skin underneath. Most tigers are orange and black to help keep them camouflaged in the rainforest, where there are lots of plants, trees, and shrubs.

A tiger's stripes help keep them hidden when they are stalking prey.

Black tear marks run from the inside corners of a cheetah's eyes, to the outside corners of its mouth.

Fur and markings

Cats are known for their stunning coats. Fur protects the skin and keeps cats warm. Coloured markings break up their outline, which helps cats blend in and hide in their surroundings. This is called camouflage. Colours and markings vary according to where each cat lives and hunts.

Rosettes

This rose-like pattern can completely cover the fur, appear in clumps, or have a spot in the centre. Dark rosettes on cream fur break up the cat's outline, making it hard to see in light and shady parts of its habitat.

Black fur

Some cats are almost entirely covered in thick, black fur. However, look closely, and you can see this black jaguar's markings are still there. Many cats hunt at night, and creep up on prey behind a cloak of darkness.

This beautiful coat acts as camouflage when the leopard is on the move.

Unsuspecting prey stand little chance when a black jaguar prepares to pounce.

WOW!

No **two tigers** look the same. **Every tiger** has its own **unique stripe pattern,** like your **fingerprints!**

Clean coats

Big cats are often seen using their rough tongues to lick themselves. This keeps the fur clean and spreads natural oil, helping keep the coat smooth. Licking the fur also keeps cats cool in the hot tropical regions where many species live.

Tiger grooming

Inside a big cat

Beneath the furry coat of a big cat lies a bony skeleton. The skeletons of big cats are very similar to one another. They share a flexible backbone, strong legs, and wide jaws. The arrangement of the bones is perfect for speedy running and skilled hunting.

Sturdy skeleton

The big cat body is held together by a framework of about 250 bones. This protects the vital organs and gives cats fast and fluid movement in the limbs. The skeleton shown here is a tiger's.

Tail
Used for balance, the huge tail measures about 1 m (3 ft) in length.

Legs
The back legs are much longer than the front legs, which makes leaping and climbing easier.

Feline features

Big cats have skeletal and muscular systems that are suited to their lifestyle. Sharp teeth and powerful muscles are essential for successful hunting.

This skull of a lion shows how wide a big cat's open jaws are.

A tiger baring its teeth

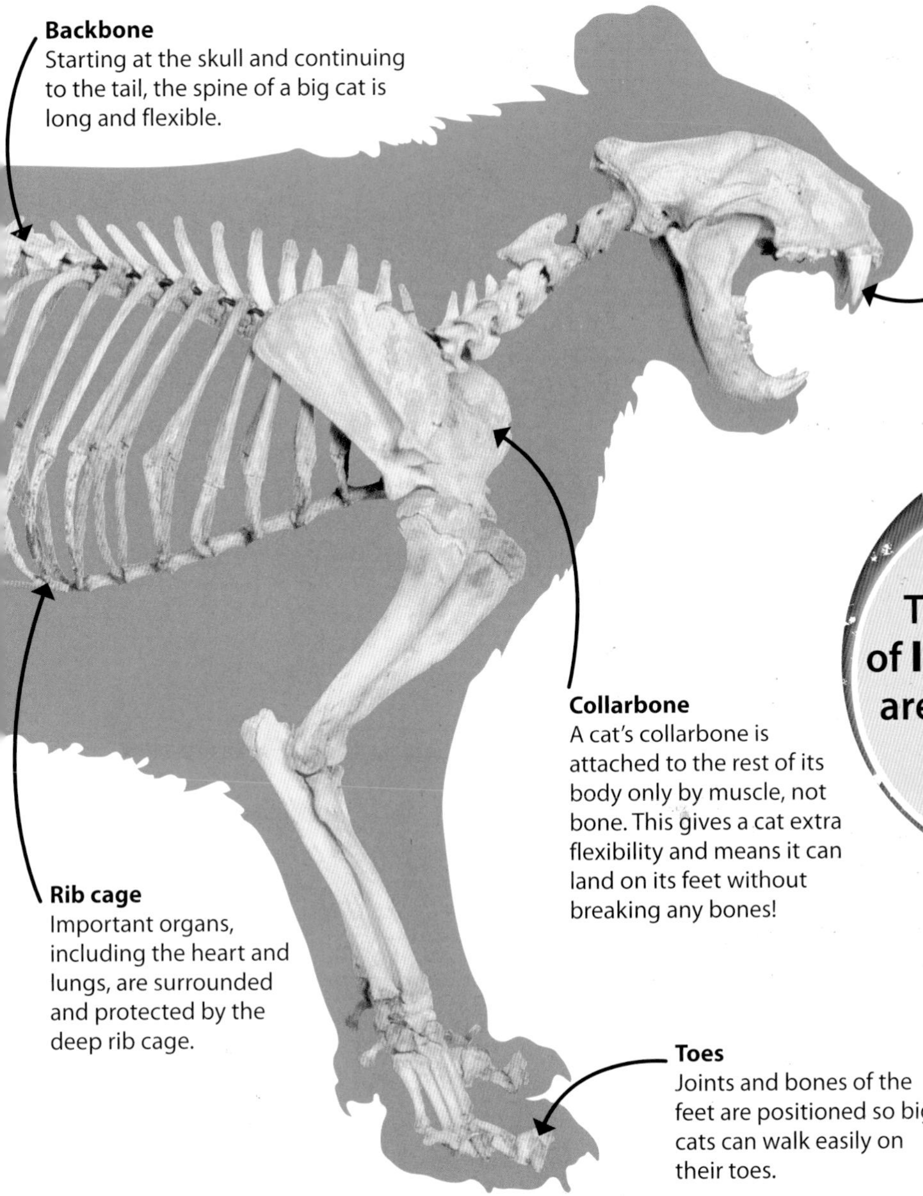

Backbone
Starting at the skull and continuing to the tail, the spine of a big cat is long and flexible.

Teeth
The wide jaw and sharp teeth are designed for hunting prey and eating every scrap of food.

! WOW!

The **skeletons** of **lions** and **tigers** are impossible to tell apart!

Collarbone
A cat's collarbone is attached to the rest of its body only by muscle, not bone. This gives a cat extra flexibility and means it can land on its feet without breaking any bones!

Rib cage
Important organs, including the heart and lungs, are surrounded and protected by the deep rib cage.

Toes
Joints and bones of the feet are positioned so big cats can walk easily on their toes.

Strong jaws
Cats have strong jaws and teeth. When eating, the jaws open up wide to help the cat break the tough bones of its prey.

A puma leaping off rocky mountains

Mighty muscles
Strong muscles in the long back legs help big cats to jump long distances and pounce on prey from high up.

Superior senses

Big cats have heightened senses, which are far better developed than ours. A big cat's senses need to work well together when hunting alone at night. Eyes closely observe surroundings, the ears detect even the slightest sound, and the nose can sniff out any creature close by.

Sight

The eyesight of a big cat is six times better than that of a human. They have big, bright eyes, but the pupils change size depending on light levels. At night, the pupils expand and light floods in, giving excellent night vision.

The pupils go much smaller in bright sunlight.

TASTE

A long, rough tongue ensures big cats can taste different prey, recognize rotten meat, and get bits of meat off the bone. Their tongues have no sweet receptors, so they are not interested in eating anything sweet!

Jacobson's organ

A special organ in the roof of the mouth allows big cats to accurately identify different scents from other cats and analyze them. They use this information to communicate with each other.

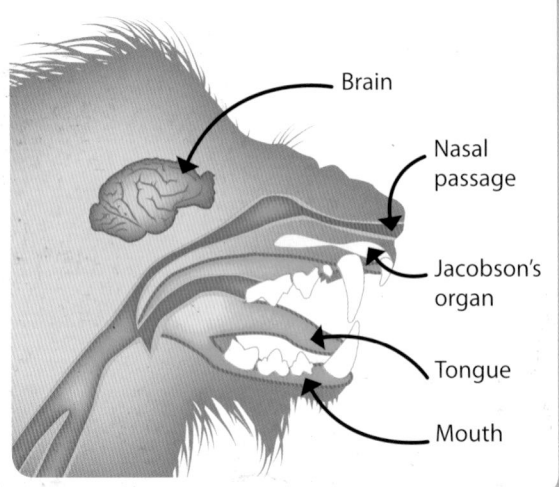

Brain

Nasal passage

Jacobson's organ

Tongue

Mouth

Smell

A cat's sensitive nose can pick up on scents over long distances. This helps big cats communicate with each other, find mates, and detect and track prey. Scents enter their nostrils and travel over smell receptors for the big cats to identify.

The nose has no fur, making it highly sensitive to smells.

SOUND

Most big cats have large, movable ears to recognize sounds and the direction they are coming from. They can identify prey by the noises they make. Cats can detect some sounds that we as humans cannot pick up.

TOUCH

Naturally cautious, big cats use their paws to feel and examine anything unfamiliar. Once they know it is safe, they use their nose and whiskers for further investigation.

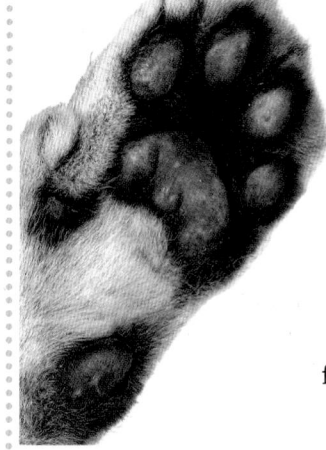

Whiskers

Whiskers are an important tool that helps the other senses. These long, stiff hairs help big cats judge the nearness of prey in the dark. They also help with biting prey. Whiskers are pulled forwards as they bite, which helps make the bite more accurate.

Whiskers have sensitive nerve-endings at the roots.

Where cats live

Cats make their homes in many natural areas, called habitats. Each species has adapted to survive in its chosen habitat. These range from snowy mountains and swampy marshlands to scorching deserts and steamy rainforests.

Habitat loss

Today, many cats are under threat in their own habitats. A great number of forests have had their trees cut down so that people can use the wood. Cutting down trees also makes space for farmland. This is called deforestation. As land is cleared, cats may lose their original territories and need to find new homes.

Deforestation of a forest

Desert
Life is tough for wild cats living in dry, barren deserts where water and food are limited. They must learn to survive for long periods of time without regular water.

Snowy mountains
The cold climates of mountain peaks and snowy forests suit some very big cats, including the Amur, or Siberian, tiger. Fur grows thicker and longer to keep them warm.

Grassland
The African grasslands are home to many big cats. Thick grass covers this habitat. However, there is not enough yearly rainfall for trees to grow.

Rainforest
Tropical rainforests are hot and very rainy. The thick green plants, flowing rivers, and mix of creatures help big cats survive and even thrive here.

Rocky mountains
Rocky mountains have high, sharp drops and tough ridges. Cats need to use their expert climbing and balancing skills to live in this landscape.

Wetlands
Parts of the world can flood in heavy rain and soon become huge wetlands. Here, lots of animals make their homes in marshes and swamps.

Caracal

"Caracal" means "black ears". This cat uses its long legs to leap into the air and catch birds in the grasslands of Africa and the Middle East.

Snow leopard

This solitary cat roams some of the highest mountains in Central Asia. It survives on a diet of goats, sheep, and hares.

Cheetah

This champion cat is faster than any other animal on Earth. It has an athletic body and long legs, which help it to hunt at breathtaking speed.

Bengal tiger

This big cat sits at the top of the food chain in the rainforests of Asia. Here, it has plenty of water to drink and lots of animals to eat.

Puma

The puma is also called a mountain lion. High up in the mountains of the Americas, it uses its powerful back legs and large claws to scramble across difficult ground.

Jaguar

This cool cat is at home in the wetlands of Central and South America. It patrols the riverbanks, hunting prey on land or in water.

Water-dwellers

Although most domestic cats hate water, some wild ones are happy to make a splash! Several species are skilled swimmers. They will enter rivers and lakes to catch prey, cool off in the hot sun, or simply enjoy a bathe.

! WOW

While **all cats can swim,** few of them choose to, and most prefer to **stay on dry land.**

FACT FILE

» **Regions:** South and Central America

» **Location:** Amazon Basin

Jaguar

The jaguar enjoys regular swims in the American tropics. Here, the many rivers and streams are a perfect hunting ground for prey ranging in size from fish to crocodiles.

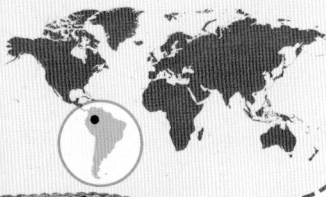

Caimans are among the preferred prey of jaguars in water.

White-tailed deer can swim across rivers and are a target for tigers.

Swimming lessons

Some cats coax their cubs into the water to help them get used to it. Cubs learn to swim by watching their mother and following what she does.

Mountain lion cub swimming

Fishing cat

This wild cat lives in the wetlands of Asia. The fishing cat is suited to living and hunting in water. It has webbed toes on its front paws.

FACT FILE

» **Regions:** India and Indonesia

» **Location:** mangrove forests of the Sundarbans

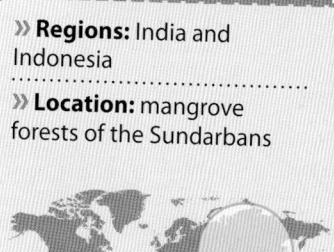

Fishing cats dive underwater and grasp fish with their sharp claws.

Tigers

The biggest of the big cats is among the strongest swimmers. However, tigers are more likely to use rivers to cool down than to hunt.

FACT FILE

» **Regions:** Asia

» **Location:** India, Siberia, and parts of Southeast Asia

Snow leopards

One of the world's rarest big cats lives a lonely existence on the snowy slopes of Central Asia. Blending in with the mountains, the nimble-footed snow leopard is able to leap and chase prey downhill. It uses its amazing strength to catch and bring down goats, sheep, and other prey.

Thick fur
Long, thick, woolly fur is necessary to keep the snow leopard warm in freezing temperatures.

Long tail
The huge, furry tail is almost half the entire length of the snow leopard. It helps with balance on rocky ground and offers a warm blanket for snuggling up to in the snow.

The mysterious cat

The secretive snow leopard is difficult to spot because of its colour and location. Because of this, it's difficult to say how many there are. Footprints in the snow, traces of wee (urine), and scratch marks on trees, all give clues about numbers.

Footprints of a snow leopard

Short ears

The ears are shorter and smaller than most big cats, which helps to reduce heat loss in the icy environment.

Nasal cavity

As the snow leopard breathes in the chilly air, the large nasal cavity (hollow space) warms it up on the way to the lungs.

Strong muscles

Lined with muscles, the powerful chest gives the snow leopard the strength to climb across rocks easily.

Padded paws

All four puffy paws are cushioned to keep the heat inside and stop the snow leopard sinking into deep snow.

A ju

Climbing cats

Trees provide a safe place for many cats. Climbing branches offers the best view of their surroundings and a great place to catnap. Cats can hide behind dense leaves. This helps them avoid predators, stalk prey, and feast on dead animals, away from hungry scavengers.

Leopard
This expert climber is the biggest cat to climb trees. Leopards carry their prey into the treetops to avoid packs of hyenas or jackals moving in to steal their food.

Top cats

Smaller cats use their light frames and sharp claws to climb trees easily. High branches offer a clear view of the grasslands and forests below.

A margay prepares to leap

Margay
Margays are small wild cats with long legs and a long tail, who leap through the trees of South America. In the forest tree tops they can find plenty of birds and squirrels to eat.

A clouded leopard views the forest below

Clouded leopard
This nimble-footed cat prowls high up in the trees of the dense forests of Southeast Asia. The clouded leopard is a secretive animal that is hard to spot. It is one of the best climbers of all cats. It can rotate (turn) its back paws and then run headfirst down a tree, like a squirrel!

! WOW!

Leopards can **carry prey** weighing nearly **twice** their own body weight!

Movement

Meet the world's fastest animal on land. This incredible cat can travel as fast as a car on the motorway while hunting prey in the African grasslands.

! WOW!

Cheetahs are the only big cat that can turn in mid-air while running!

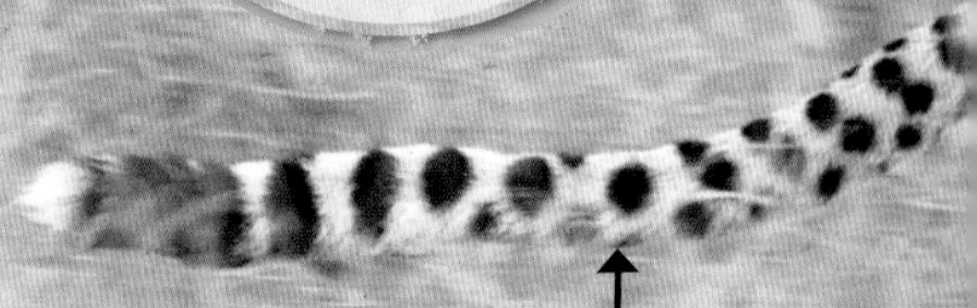

The long, flat tail works like a boat's rudder, allowing the cheetah to turn faster and keep its balance when sprinting.

Safe landing

The saying goes that cats have nine lives. Although this is not true, they are great at jumping and landing safely. Cats have an in-built righting reflex that helps them to turn in mid-air and fall on their feet.

During a fall, the cat first levels its head ready to turn.

The cat rotates its chest and front legs to turn the right way around.

The back legs turn and straighten out in preparation to hit the ground.

Now fully flipped over, the four feet can absorb the shock on landing.

Full stretch

Together, a cheetah's bendy spine and long legs enable it to make huge strides with all four feet off the ground.

The long spine keeps the body flexible and athletic.

Coiled spring
The flexible spine works like a coiled spring, storing up energy before releasing it as the cheetah starts to sprint.

The head stays steady and focused on the prey during the hunt.

Cheetahs have longer legs than most big cats.

Pride of lions

Sociable lions are the only big cats to live in groups, called prides. Each family member has its own role to fulfil. Lions communicate by roaring, growling, and licking each other. Prides live freely on African grasslands, with no natural predators but plenty of prey to target and eat.

! WOW!

A **dark mane** makes the lion **more attractive** to lionesses!

Lion

A male lion's job is to defend the pride's territory. There are only one or two males in most prides. They roar loudly and use scent-marking to warn off other males.

Lioness

Females outnumber the males in every pride. Hardworking lionesses do most of the hunting, and care for their young. Every two years a lioness gives birth to a litter of up to five cubs.

Cubs

The average pride has about 12 cubs. They learn to hunt by watching the lionesses in action. Cubs play-fight and give chase, helping them grow in strength and confidence.

Mane attraction

The majestic mane of the lion shows its power and position in the pride. A thick mane also makes the lion appear larger to other males. Lionesses do not have manes, as this would weigh them down when hunting.

Lioness and lion

On a hunt

As darkness falls on the African savannah, lionesses gather in groups to plan the night's work. With meat on their minds, they must work as a team to ensure the pride does not go hungry.

The adult lionesses wait until night falls to start their organised operation. This time of day is much cooler, so they use less energy.

On spotting prey, by sight or sound, lionesses lie low. Then they start to move towards their target, slowly and silently...

The younger lionesses give chase first. They are the speediest and strongest. This teamwork is a strength of lion prides, who are not the fastest of the big cats. The prey – a large group of zebras – run away, fast...

The young lionesses isolate one zebra and start to gather round it. The older and more experienced lionesses are lying in wait, ready to pounce.

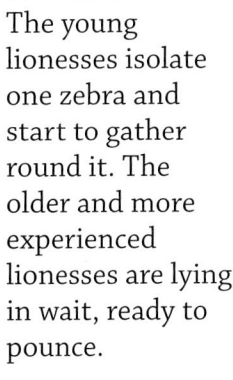

The lionesses attack! They bring the zebra to the ground. They bite into the zebra's flesh. The lone zebra has no chance against so many lions. Even very large prey are a potential kill when outnumbered by attackers.

Now the feeding hierarchy gets underway. If the lion is present, he must feast first. The cubs join him later, before the lionesses get the leftovers. A large kill satisfies the pride for a week before another hunt begins.

Night prowlers

Most cats don't waste time sleeping at night! Many are up and about, using the darkness to their advantage. These action-packed hours see cats hunting and feeding. Animals that are awake at night and sleep in the day are called nocturnal. Nocturnal activities are possible because big cats can see just as well at night as they do in the day, but unsuspecting prey cannot see them.

! WOW!

A big cat on the **hunt** was recorded travelling more than **40 km (25 miles)** in one night!

Hunting at night

Midnight feast
After a successful hunt, this leopard has dragged its prey up into a tree to eat. Being high up keeps the food away from other animals that may smell the dead animal and move in.

Bright eyes
Like all wild cats, the eyes of this sand cat appear to glow in the dark. A special reflective layer absorbs as much light as possible into the back of the eyes.

Light-reflecting eyes

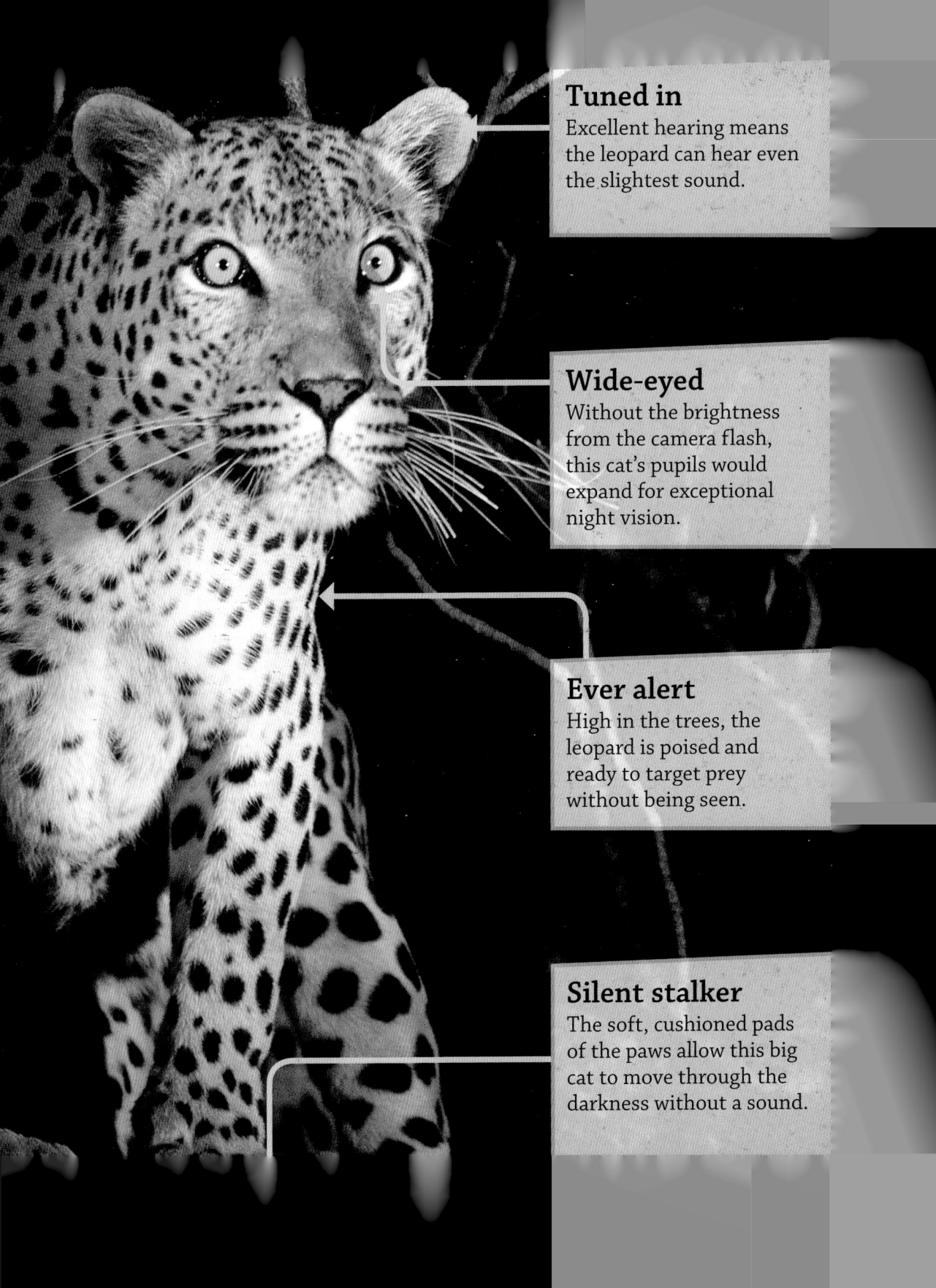

Tuned in
Excellent hearing means the leopard can hear even the slightest sound.

Wide-eyed
Without the brightness from the camera flash, this cat's pupils would expand for exceptional night vision.

Ever alert
High in the trees, the leopard is poised and ready to target prey without being seen.

Silent stalker
The soft, cushioned pads of the paws allow this big cat to move through the darkness without a sound.

Cat sounds

Big cats and other wild cats communicate in a variety of ways and always make themselves heard. From grunting and growling to hissing and snarling, these sounds can be signs of aggression or happiness, or simple forms of communication with other cats or wild animals.

Growl

Watch out! Tigers and other big cats often growl as the first sign of aggression. This warns other animals that an attack is likely unless they leave or retreat.

Chirrup

Among the softest speakers of the cat world, cheetahs cannot roar. Instead they produce a distinctive chirruping sound to show affection or attract a mate.

Purr

Pumas purr just like domestic cats and kittens. Purring is a sign of satisfaction or affection. It can also be the sound of a mother bonding with her cubs.

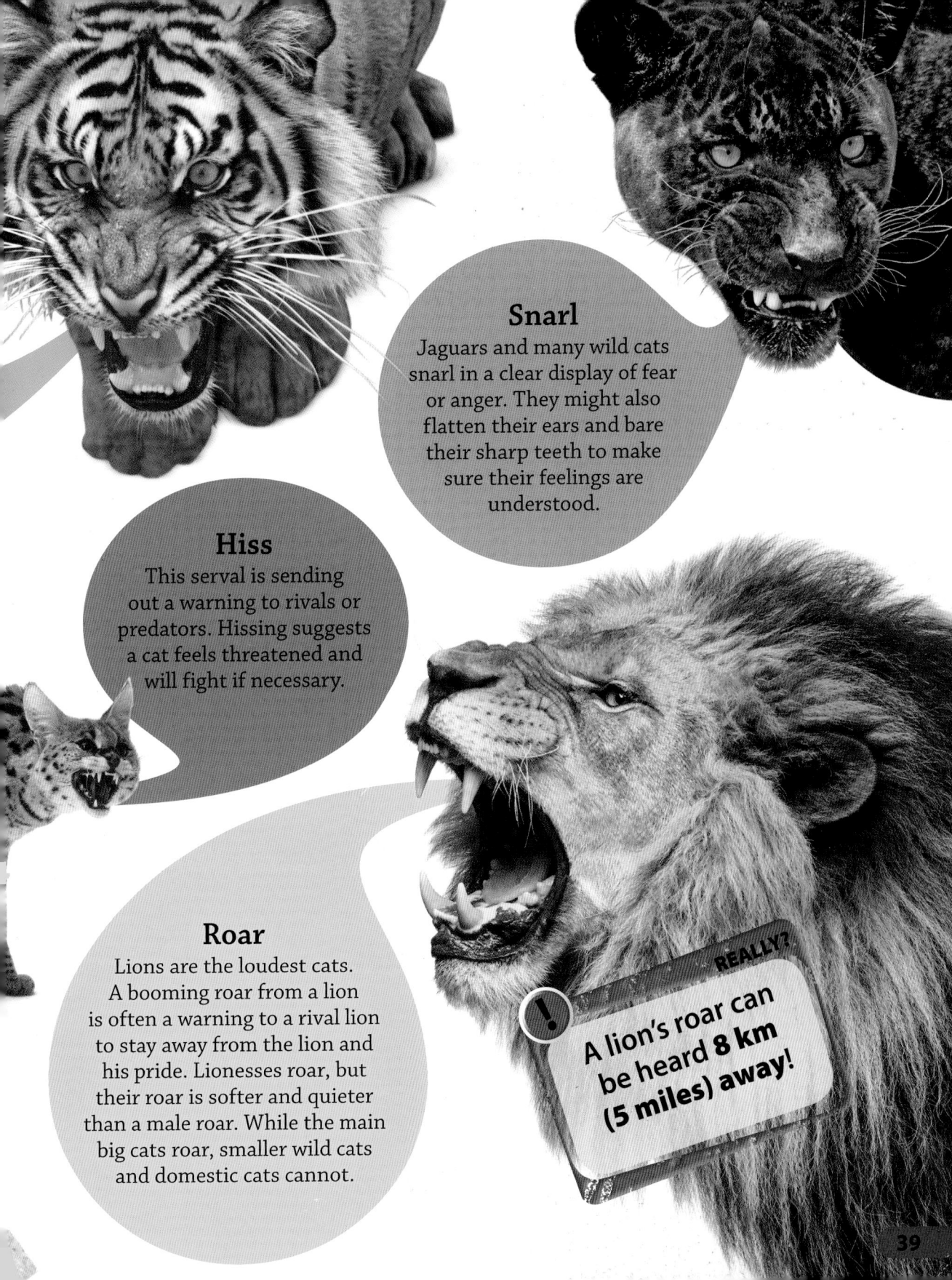

Snarl

Jaguars and many wild cats snarl in a clear display of fear or anger. They might also flatten their ears and bare their sharp teeth to make sure their feelings are understood.

Hiss

This serval is sending out a warning to rivals or predators. Hissing suggests a cat feels threatened and will fight if necessary.

Roar

Lions are the loudest cats. A booming roar from a lion is often a warning to a rival lion to stay away from the lion and his pride. Lionesses roar, but their roar is softer and quieter than a male roar. While the main big cats roar, smaller wild cats and domestic cats cannot.

REALLY?

A lion's roar can be heard **8 km (5 miles)** away!

Tigers

The tiger is the world's largest and heaviest big cat. There are five types (called subspecies) of tiger, and they all live in Asia. Whether living in tropical rainforest or snow-covered woodland, they all depend on forest habitats, which provide water and food for survival.

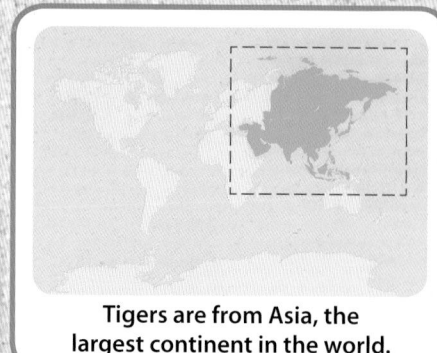

Tigers are from Asia, the largest continent in the world.

India

A group of Bengal tigers

Bengal tiger
Bengal tigers live mostly in India. There are more Bengal tigers than any other type of tiger. Some live in mangrove forest swamps called the Sundarbans. However, the destruction of forests and illegal hunting mean there are now fewer Bengal tigers than ever before.

Indochinese tiger
At home in Southeast Asia, the Indochinese tiger uses its powerful legs to run and swim after prey. Its stripy coat gives it great camouflage – helping it hide behind trees before pouncing.

An Indochinese tiger

Amur tiger

The Amur tiger, also known as the Siberian tiger, is the largest of the big cats and lives in the coldest climate. Having the longest, thickest fur coat helps this tiger to stay warm during snowy Siberian winters.

A Siberian tiger in the Sikhote-Alin mountain range

Russia

Vietnam

Malaysia

Indonesia

A Malayan tiger in wetland habitat

Malayan tiger

This small tiger roams the forests of south Thailand and west Malaysia. It hunts deer, boar, and goats in leafy forests, and enjoys swimming in wetlands.

Sumatran tiger

The Sumatran tiger lives on the Indonesian island of Sumatra. The smallest tiger in the world, this big cat measures 30 per cent smaller and weighs 50 per cent less than the biggest big cat, the Siberian tiger.

A Sumatran tiger resting

Catnaps

Big cats spend much of their time asleep. This isn't because they are lazy, but because they don't want to waste energy. They prefer lots of short power naps to one big sleep. In hot countries, the daylight hours of scorching sunshine are best for sleeping, leaving dawn, dusk, and night-time for hunting.

Sleep sites

Wild cats must consider where is best to sleep. Cool places offer protection from the heat, while sheltered spots are perfect hideaways from rivals or predators.

A lazy leopard napping on a tree branch

Shady snooze
Trees offer a welcome retreat for tired leopards. Here they can nap high in the branches, away from prying eyes.

Lounging lions

Lion prides like to sleep in the shade of trees. Lions are at the top of the food chain, so they have no predators.

! WOW!

Big cats in the wild can **sleep** or **rest** for more than **18 hours** a day!

Solitary sleep
Any lion without an established pride is vulnerable. They must stay fully awake longer, or rest with one eye open to watch for signs of danger.

A lion rests with one eye open to look out for danger

Marking territories

Many cats create their own areas, called territories, and adopt different ways to mark them. Territories vary in size, but need to contain enough prey for the cats to hunt. Boundaries are marked to warn other cats to stay away, but if a rival strays into another territory, fights can result.

Scratching

Like most big cats, lions love scratching tree trunks. This cleans and sharpens their claws, and keeps them in good condition. It also marks their territory with a scent, so other cats can tell where they have been.

Vocalizing

From this hissing serval to the roaring lion, wild cats use aggressive noises to scare enemies away. Spitting and gritting teeth are two other ways that cats keep territories clear of rivals.

Cub care

Male big cats may attack and kill the cubs of rival males in the fight to win a mate. Females try to protect their young by taking them away from the danger zone, and create a safe den in which to raise them. They carry cubs gently by the nape (back) of their necks and hide them in thick foliage (plants) for safety.

A female leopard carrying her cub

Scenting

This cheetah is marking its territory with scent marks to warn that the area is already taken. Its scent is mixed with urine (wee). It is sprayed over territory lines and trees to stop rivals from crossing territory borders. The scent can last for weeks.

Fighting over turf

Tigers are one of many types of big cat that will fight to keep control of a territory. Competition for the same mate can also cause aggressive fights between cats.

Playtime

It can't be all work and no play for big cats! In between time spent hunting, sleeping, and eating, they entertain themselves and form friendships. Cubs in particular love to play. They grow in confidence by copying adult behaviour and learn essential survival techniques, too.

Tree climbing

Cubs learn how to climb trees by following their mothers. This is for fun while cats are young, but becomes an important survival skill in later life.

Play-fighting

Young cubs enjoy play-fighting together, which helps build physical strength, encourages self-protection, and teaches hunting techniques.

Tail play

Playful cubs practise giving chase by trying to catch their mother's tails. This speeds up their reactions in preparation for chasing live prey.

Rolling

A happy big cat rolls around on its back, enjoying the freedom and relaxation. By revealing his tummy, this lion shows he feels secure in his pride.

Swimming

Tigers are strong swimmers and will often take a dip to cool off or just for their own enjoyment.

Rubbing

Big cats show affection by rubbing and licking each other's heads. This process exchanges individual scents and strengthens social bonds.

Grooming

Big cats see grooming as a sociable activity and take time to clean each other's fur. This helps them identify one another by their scent. Mothers keep their cubs clean using their rough tongues to remove dirt and tangles.

Meet the expert

Giles Clark is the director of Big Cats and Conservation at The Big Cat Sanctuary in Kent, England. The sanctuary houses over 50 cats, and supports conservation projects overseas.

Q: We know it is something to do with cats, but what is your actual job?

A: Firstly, I help my team look after our cats here at The Big Cat Sanctuary. This means making sure we take care of all their needs and keep them active. Secondly, I help oversee education programmes – spreading awareness about endangered animals is an important part of my job. Finally, I help decide how we can assist conservation projects and programmes working to save wild cats and their natural habitats.

Q: What made you want to work with cats?

A: Some of my earliest and fondest memories growing up as a young boy are of the many domestic cats my parents used to take in and rescue. Some of these cats were my first friends, and it was being around them that allowed me to develop a passion and respect for all cats – big and small!

Q: What is it about big cats that you love?

A: I find all cats fascinating. There are 40 species of cats that have spanned almost the entire planet, all with similar characteristics and traits, and yet each species is unique and perfectly adapted to its own environment at the same time. Domestic cats are the most popular pet in the world, and if you watch how they live in your house and garden, you will see many behaviours they have that are very similar to their wild cousins.

Q: Why are big cats important?

Cats are such a vital part of the ecosystems where they live. Big cats are at the top of the food chain and help maintain a healthy balance in nature. To save these magnificent

Giles with a Sumatran tiger and cub at Australia Zoo, Queensland, Australia

species, we must protect their habitats. In turn this will save all the other species that live in the same habitats, from the smallest of insects to primates in the trees. Cats kept in zoos and sanctuaries help scientists learn and understand more about these species. This knowledge can be used to help cats in the wild and help awareness of conservation issues.

Q: Do you have a favourite species of cat?

A: It's almost impossible for me to choose a favourite species of cat! I have spent many years looking after tigers, so will always have a special place for them in my heart. Equally, the clouded leopard is another species that I find absolutely incredible.

Q: Do you have any cats of your own?

A: I have always had cats at home and sometimes not always domestic cats! Over the years I have been required to hand-raise several cubs that have needed special care and attention, most recently a baby jaguar called Maya who was only six days old when

Giles with Maya the jaguar

she arrived. Like her mum would have, I fed her through the night for the first few months. I did this until she was about three months old and strong enough to live back at the sanctuary. Wild animals don't make good pets though – they can be dangerous when they start to grow up.

Q: What is the most difficult part of your job?

A: Saying goodbye to some of the cats I have cared for is always very difficult. The other thing I find very hard is knowing that so many species of cats are endangered, and risk becoming extinct in the wild because of humans and our actions.

Q: What is the best thing about your job?

A: The best part of my job is knowing that I get to make a difference, not only improving the lives of the cats I help look after but also helping to protect them in the wild. I always get excited talking to people about how important it is to protect our natural world and all the amazing species we share the planet with. For a long time, humans have been part of the problem for cats in the wild, but now we can be part of the solution!

Playing with a serval

Under threat

Today, the number of cats in the wild has reduced dramatically to very low levels. People are ultimately to blame, from hunting wild cats to destroying their homes. The growing world population has affected the environment and changed natural habitats forever, causing wild cats and their prey to face an ongoing struggle for survival.

Deforestation

Big cats, including tigers and jaguars, have seen their habitats disappear when people cut down trees and clear the land. Large areas of forest have been destroyed.

Deforestation in the Amazon rainforest, Brazil

Further farmland

Many areas of forest and grassland have been turned into farmland, leaving less space for wild cats. As jaguars and cheetahs have attacked farm animals, farmers set traps to stop them.

Illegal trade

Sadly, in some countries today, the illegal buying and selling of animal fur and bones is still taking place. Tigers and cheetahs are among the victims of these illegal hunters.

High-profile campaigns have highlighted the cruelty in wearing animal fur.

Snow leopards are forced to move higher up the mountains as people move in.

Trophy hunting

Hunters consider lions the top prize. Although laws have been introduced to protect wild cats, illegal hunting continues.

Population explosion

With the world population increasing, there is less room for wild cats than before. Their habitats shrink to make room for more housing for humans.

Limited prey

Wild cats are facing a reduced food supply. They must compete with other animals for the same prey. People hunt the prey of wild cats, which also leads to them having less food.

Animals such as antelopes are a target for many meat-eaters (carnivores).

Endangered or extinct?

When a big cat species reduces in number, it is given a rank to describe the threat level and how likely a species is to become extinct in the future. Threatened species are given the rank of vulnerable, endangered, or critically endangered, according to how high the threat level is. If a species dies out completely it is called extinct.

The American lion became extinct 11,000 years ago.

How we're helping

Today, there are many ways in which we can help to protect big cats and aid their survival. Conservation efforts are underway around the world to help boost the numbers of big cats. Some big cats live in protected areas, and new laws are being introduced to stop hunting.

Trained staff work closely alongside the big cats.

A keeper training a cheetah

Sanctuaries

Keeping big cats in animal sanctuaries means that they are sure of a regular food supply, are safe from human hunters, and enjoy a longer life expectancy. Sanctuaries and safari parks also use breeding programmes to increase their numbers, with some cats being released back into the wild.

The Big Cat Sanctuary in Kent, England, holds more than 50 cats.

REALLY?

In **2016,** tiger numbers **increased** for the first time in a century.

Anti-poaching laws

The introduction of new laws to ban hunting and poaching has helped to protect the world's big cats. Further measures have been taken to enforce the bans and deter illegal hunting.

Educating

Teaching children about big cats and conservation in local schools is an important way of encouraging future generations to play their part in protecting the planet's wildlife.

A conservationist teaching a class in South Africa

Lessons on conservation show children how to live alongside and help wildlife.

Tracking cats

Keeping track of big cats helps conservationists understand the threats facing them. A Global Positioning System (GPS) collar reveals a big cat's movements and what they do.

A GPS collar helps track a cat's movements and is completely harmless.

Conservation projects

Many conservation projects focus on replanting trees to rebuild natural habitats and encourage big cats to return.

Anti-poaching dogs protect Kenya's endangered wildlife.

A community in the Amazon rainforest planting tree seedlings

BASTET

In Ancient Egypt, cats were worshipped as gods and any ill-treatment of one could be punishable by death. Bastet was an Egyptian goddess whose symbol was the cat. The goddess was believed to protect those who worshipped her.

JAGUARS

The jaguar featured in Aztec and Maya cultures in Mexico and Central America. Aztec warriors dressed as jaguars as they believed it would give them strength and provide protection when fighting a war.

Legends

Throughout history, cats have played an important part in the culture and religion of many countries around the world. In some societies, such as Ancient Egypt, cats have been worshipped as gods. It's been said that cats have a mysterious, aloof quality, or aura. Perhaps it's this that has captured the hearts and minds of people for centuries, and continues to do so today.

DAWON

In Hindu religious mythology in India, Dawon was a terrifying tiger who symbolized power. The goddess Durga would ride Dawon into battle. While Durga fought with weapons, Dawon used its claws and teeth.

HAECHI

The lion has long been seen as a protector in Asia. This big cat featured in Indian and Chinese art before reaching Korea. Here it was named Haechi and carved in wood and stone sculptures.

Good fortune

Cats are considered lucky in many places. The Maneki-neko, or "Beckoning cat", remains a lucky talisman in Japan. A raised right paw means good luck, while the left means welcome. The Buddhist faith, based on the teachings of the Buddha, also holds cats in high esteem. Buddhists believe that when a person dies, their soul goes to a cat for safekeeping.

Maneki-neko

The Buddha with three big cats

Ancient ancestors

The first wild cats stalked this planet many millions of years ago. The discovery of fossils has helped us to understand ancient cats. Fossils show us that in many ways, ancient cats were similar to modern big cats, but that over time, big cats have developed sharp teeth and claws, two important features that they can't live without today.

» Scale

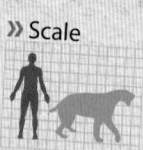

Miacis

A fossil discovered in Germany revealed a cat that looked like a long-legged weasel. Miacis lived about 56–34 million years ago. It was an excellent climber that used its long tail for balancing on tree branches.

» Scale

Xenosmilus

This powerful cat lived in North America around one million years ago. Its heavy weight put a stop to fast hunting, so instead, Xenosmilus used trees for cover before pouncing on passing prey, including wild pigs.

Dinictis

The same size as a serval, Dinictis prowled the grasslands of North America looking for prey around 34–20 million years ago. While today most cats walk on their toes, a fossil found in South Dakota proved this ancient cat was very flat-footed.

» Scale

The **oldest fossils** relating to the **cat family** are **50 million years old!**

Beneath its soft fur and small skull, Dinictis hid dagger-like canine teeth.

Smilodon

Snarling Smilodon is known for its gaping fangs. Meaning "sword", sabre-toothed cats used their terrific teeth to stab huge prey, including mammoth and bison. Like modern-day lions, sociable Smilodon lived and hunted in groups before becoming extinct about 12,000 years ago.

» Scale

Smilodon teeth could reach 50 cm (20 in) in length and never stopped growing!

Big cat facts and figures

Big cats are among the fastest and strongest animals, and the most successful carnivores on Earth. Read on for some cat facts to really sink your teeth into...

Of all the cats, **servals** have the **biggest ears** and **legs** compared to the rest of their **body**.

No big cat species is **indigenous** (originates in) to the continent of **Australia**.

A cheetah can reach **112 kph (70 mph)** in just **3 seconds**.

10 CM

A lion's canine tooth, including the root, is 10 cm (4 in) long compared to an adult human's canine, which is only 1.5 cm (½ in) long.

50%

About half of all species of wild cats are vulnerable, endangered, or critically endangered.

The word "**jaguar**" is derived from the Native American word "**yaguar**", which means "**he who kills with one leap**".

The male lions of **TSAVO** in Kenya **have short and tufty manes**, like a bad haircut!

A **jaguar's jaws** are strong enough to crack open tortoise shells – helping it get to one of its favourite treats.

250KG

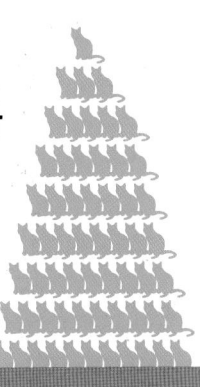

The average male Siberian tiger weighs 250 kg (550 lb) – that's more than 60 domestic cats!

2,500

The approximate number of spots on an adult cheetah.

Glossary

Here are the meanings of some words that are useful for you to know when learning all about big cats.

accelerate Speed up

ambush Unexpected attack from a hidden position

apex predator Predator at the top of the food chain

aquatic Living in water

camouflage Colours or patterns on an animal's skin or fur that helps it blend in with its surroundings

canine Large, pointed tooth belonging to a mammal

captivity State of being confined or enclosed, and prevented from escaping

carnivore Animal that eats meat

conservation Saving the environment, which includes attempts to protect endangered animals and stop them from becoming extinct

cranium Area of the skull protecting the brain

cub The young of wild animals, such as lions, cheetahs, or tigers

deforestation The cutting down of a forest or large expanse of trees

domesticated Animals kept as pets, or living on farms

ecosystem Plants and animals that live in an area, and the relationship that exists between them and their habitat

endangered Species low in numbers that could become extinct

environment Surroundings in which an animal lives

extinct When a species dies out so none are left in the world

feline Member of the cat family

feral Animal living wild that was once domesticated or in captivity

food chain Series of living things in which each thing feeds on the next one

fossil Remains of a dead animal that has become embedded in rock and preserved over time

A puma is a large and powerful carnivore.

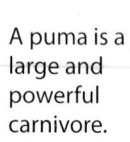

habitat Natural home environment of an animal

indigenous Originating or occurring naturally in a particular place

instinct An animal's natural response to a situation

kill Animal or animals killed during a hunt

lineage Generations of the same family

mammal Warm-blooded, vertebrate animals that have skin covered in hair. Females feed their young milk

migration Movement of people or animals from one place to another

naturalist Expert in the scientific study of animals or plants

nocturnal Animal that is active at night to hunt or feed

poaching Illegal hunting of wild animals

predator Animal that naturally hunts other living animals for food

prey Animal that is hunted and killed for food

pride Family group of lions

rainforest Thick forest of tall trees and other vegetation that is found in tropical areas

reproduce To have young

retractable Something that can be drawn back, for example, claws

rival Animal competing for the same territory or mate

sanctuary Safe haven from danger

savannah Area of grassland with few trees

scavenger Animal that feeds on the remains of another animal that is already dead

scent Individual smell produced by an animal

senses Sight, smell, hearing, taste, and touch are senses

sociable Friendly interaction with other members of the same species

solitary Animal that lives alone

species A group of plants or animals that all share similar features or characteristics

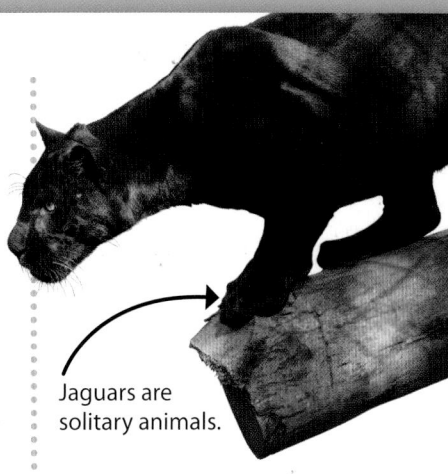

Jaguars are solitary animals.

subspecies A smaller group within a species that have specific features and a shared location

territory Area that is defended by an animal

tropical Area or climate with hot temperatures and high rainfall

vegetation Plant life found in a particular habitat

vertebrate Animal with a backbone

vulnerable Species likely to become endangered unless threats to its survival reduce

warm-blooded Animal that keeps a constant body temperature

Index

Acknowledgements

DORLING KINDERSLEY would like to thank: Polly Goodman for proofreading, Helen Peters for compiling the index, Richard Leeney for photography, and Dan Crisp for illustrations. The publishers would also like to thank Tanith Brown and the team at The Big Cat Sanctuary, and Giles Clark for the "Meet the Expert" interview and consultancy.

The publisher would like to thank the following for their kind permission to reproduce their photographs:

(Key: a-above; b-below/bottom; c-centre; f-far; l-left; r-right; t-top)

1 Dreamstime.com: Isselee (c). **3 Alamy Stock Photo:** VPC Animals Photo (bc). **Getty Images:** Anup Shah (bl). **The Big Cat Sanctuary, UK:** (crb). **4 123RF.com:** Anan Kaewkhammul / anankkml (ca, c). **The Big Cat Sanctuary, UK:** (cra). **4-5 Dorling Kindersley:** Wildlife Heritage Foundation, Kent, UK (c). **5 Dreamstime.com:** Isselee (cr). **6 123RF.com:** Thorsten Nilson (r). **7 123RF.com:** Ana Vasileva / ABV. **8 Dreamstime.com:** Isselee (bl). **9 123RF.com:** Anan Kaewkhammul / anankkml (cl); Anan Kaewkhammul (t). **Dorling Kindersley:** Wildlife Heritage Foundation, Kent, UK (bl). **10 Alamy Stock Photo:** Julie Mowbray. **11 The Big Cat Sanctuary, UK:** (tr). **13 Alamy Stock Photo:** VPC Animals Photo (c). **Dreamstime.com:** Eastmanphoto (t). **14 Dorling Kindersley:** Wildlife Heritage Foundation, Kent, UK (cla). **Fotolia:** Kevin Moore (cl). **15 Alamy Stock Photo:** Redmond Durrell (cra, cr). **Dorling Kindersley:** Wildlife Heritage Foundation, Kent, UK (cla, cl). **16 iStockphoto.com:** Freder (br). **17 Dreamstime.com:** Outdoorsman (bc). **18 Dorling Kindersley:** Wildlife Heritage Foundation, Kent, UK (t, br). **21 Ardea:** M. Watson (ca). **Depositphotos Inc:** Nicunickie1 (cb). **FLPA:** Chris Brunskill (bc); Sebastian Kennerknecht / Minden Pictures (cb/Mountain Lion). **iStockphoto.com:** Ajlber (t). **naturepl.com:** Peter Blackwell (ca/Cheetah resting). **22 123RF.com:** Johnny Lye (cl). **Dreamstime.com:** Mikael Males (bc). **22-23 Dreamstime.com:** Tony Northrup / Acanonguy (bc). **23 123RF.com:** Ondrej Prosicky (b). **Alamy Stock Photo:** Arco Images GmbH (tr). **24-25 Getty Images:** Don Johnston. **25 iStockphoto.com:** Koonyongyut (tr). **26 iStockphoto.com:** GlobalP (c). **naturepl.com:** Staffan Widstrand (br). **27 123RF.com:** Nico Smit (br). **Alamy Stock Photo:** Beata Aldridge (bl). **iStockphoto.com:** GlobalP (c). **28-29 Rex by Shutterstock:** imageBROKER. **29 Alamy Stock Photo:** Bill Attwell (crb). **iStockphoto.com:** KeithSzafranski (cra). **30 Alamy Stock Photo:** Juniors Bildarchiv GmbH (l). **30-31 naturepl.com:** Andy Rouse (t, b). **32-33 FLPA:** Edward Myles. **36 Alamy Stock Photo:** AfriPics.com (cl); Malcolm Schuyl (bc). **36-37 Alamy Stock Photo:** David Cantrille. **38 123RF.com:** Wavebreak Media Ltd (bl). **39 Alamy Stock Photo:** Amazon-Images (tr); Life on white (br). **Dreamstime.com:** Richie Lomba (tl). **40 iStockphoto.com:** Guenterguni (clb); David O'Brien (br). **40-41 Dreamstime.com:** Piotr Adamowicz / Simpson333 (Background). **41 Dreamstime.com:** Seread (tc); Sharkphoto (b). **42-43 naturepl.com:** Anup Shah. **42 Alamy Stock Photo:** Jez Bennett (bc). **43 Alamy Stock Photo:** Graham Prentice (bl). **44 Getty Images:** Hoberman Collection / UIG (r); hphimagelibrary (l). **45 123RF.com:** Simon Eeman (tr). **Getty Images:** Anup Shah (br). **iStockphoto.com:** Richmatts (l). **46 123RF.com:** Andrey Gudkov (cla). **Alamy Stock Photo:** Avalon / Photoshot License (c); André Gilden (b). **47 Alamy Stock Photo:** Safari_Pics (t). **Dreamstime.com:** Appfind (b); Villiers Steyn (b). **iStockphoto.com:** RolfSt (cr). **48 Giles Clark:** (bl). **The Big Cat Sanctuary, UK:** (tr). **49 The Big Cat Sanctuary, UK:** (tr, bl). **51 Science Photo Library:** Mark Hallett Paleoart (br). **52-53 Getty Images:** Liza van Devente / Foto24 / Gallo Images (b). **53 Alamy Stock Photo:** imageBROKER (cr); Edward Parker (br). **FLPA:** Sebastian Kennerknecht / Minden Pictures (cla). **54 Dreamstime.com:** Gator (tl); Piotr Pawinski (tr). **55 Alamy Stock Photo:** Godong (br). **Dreamstime.com:** Zatletic (tl). **56 Dreamstime.com:** Ccat82 (b/Background). **Science Photo Library:** Michael Long (cl). **57 Dreamstime.com:** Ccat82 (t/Background, crb/Background). **Science Photo Library:** DEAGOSTINI / UIG (cla); Spencer Sutton (crb/Cat); Javier Trueba / MSF (bl). **58 Dorling Kindersley:** Blackpool Zoo, Lancashire, UK (br). **Dreamstime.com:** Tony Campbell (bl). **58-59 Dreamstime.com:** Rgbe (c). **59 Alamy Stock Photo:** Octavio Campos Salles (tl); Matt Berlin: (tr). **The Big Cat Sanctuary, UK:** (ftr). **62 Dorling Kindersley:** Wildlife Heritage Foundation, Kent, UK (tl). **63 Alamy Stock Photo:** Life on white (br).

Endpaper images: *Front:* **Ardea:** Nick Gordon cb; **Dreamstime.com:** Isselee fbr, Geoffrey Kuchera br, Lukas Blazek / Lukyslukys c, cb (Pallas's cat), Rafael Angel Irusta Machin / Broker cb (Lynx); **The Big Cat Sanctuary, UK:** cb (Puma), bc; *Back:* **Dorling Kindersley:** Wildlife Heritage Foundation, Kent, UK tc, crb; **Dreamstime.com:** Geoffrey Kuchera tl; **The Big Cat Sanctuary, UK:** cl, bl, cra, bc

Cover images: *Front:* **Dreamstime.com:** Hel080808 cra, Isselee l, cb, br, Boleslaw Kubica cr; *Back:* **123RF.com:** Ana Vasileva / ABV cr; *Front Flap:* **Alamy Stock Photo:** Avalon / Photoshot License br, Life on white cr, Julie Mowbray cl; **Dreamstime.com:** Gator bl/ (2); **Fotolia:** Kevin Moore clb; **Getty Images:** Don Johnston cra; **Science Photo Library:** Javier Trueba / MSF bc; **The Big Cat Sanctuary, UK:** bl, cra/ (2); *Back Flap:* **Dorling Kindersley:** Natural History Museum, London cb/ (Gemstone), The University of Aberdeen tl; **NASA:** cb

All other images © Dorling Kindersley
For further information see:
www.dkimages.com